Golf Rules in Pictures

NEW AND REVISED EDITION

Golf Rules in Pictures

Illustrated by George Kraynak

AN OFFICIAL PUBLICATION OF
The United States Golf Association®

A PERIGEE BOOK

Perigee Books
are published by
The Putnam Publishing Group
200 Madison Avenue
New York, NY 10016

Library of Congress Cataloging-in-Publication Data

United States Golf Association.
Golf rules in pictures.

"An official publication of the United States Golf
Association."
Includes complete text of the Rules of golf as approved
by The United States Golf Association and The Royal
and Ancient Golf Club of St. Andrews.
1. Golf—Rules. I. Kraynak, George. II. Royal and
Ancient Golf Club of St. Andrews. III. United States
Golf Association. Rules of golf. 1988. IV. Title.
GV971.U5   1988   796.352′02′022   87-32882
ISBN 0-399-51438-4

Typeset by Fisher Composition, Inc.

Printed in the United States of America
11   12   13   14   15   16   17   18   19   20

Contents

Introduction

The Rules of Golf are not engraved in granite. In fact, like most rules and laws, they are subject to constant review and frequent interpretation.

The two governing bodies of the game—the United States Golf Association and the Royal and Ancient Golf Club of St. Andrews, Scotland—long ago recognized the need to have a unified set of Rules. There have been uniform Rules worldwide since 1952.

The USGA and the R&A write *The Rules of Golf* and have a combined "Decisions" service to interpret them. The Rules serve as the laws of our game, and the Decisions serve as legal precedents.

While a knowledge of the Rules and Decisions may not help you play better golf, such knowledge can certainly enhance your enjoyment of the game and may even speed up your play.

I feel that I know the Rules quite well, but I still always carry a Rules book in my bag or pocket and have been a subscriber to the USGA's Decisions Service for many years. In fact, several Rules situations that came up during tournaments involving me directly or indirectly have resulted in some of those decisions being written or rules being redefined.

I like to think, too, that my knowledge of the Rules—and a bit of reasonable stubbornness—played an important part in my first Masters victory. I was heading for that championship in 1958 as I played the par-three 12th hole in the final round.

My tee shot flew the green and plugged in the soft ground between the putting surface and a bunker. The Rules official on the scene told me that I had no relief coming and must play the ball as it lay. I was not able to convince him that a Local Rule established for that round because of general wet conditions caused by a heavy overnight rain afforded me a free drop, so I informed him that I would play a second ball taking a drop and appealed his decision to the Committee. I took a five with the embedded ball, but three with the second ball, my appeal was upheld and I eventually won that Masters by a single stroke.

The average player may not have time to study the Rules book and learn every nuance of the 34 Rules it contains. After all, not everybody makes a living playing golf!

But it does make sense to know the Rules of the game. That's why I was pleased when I was asked to write an introduction to *Golf Rules in Pictures,* which has been designed and written to give the reader a working knowledge of the Rules.

The first Rules of Golf were written in Edinburgh, Scotland, more than 240 years ago. While there have been great changes in the game over the years, the three basic principles still apply: play the ball as it lies, play the course as you find it, and when it's not possible to do either, do what's fair.

This book should help you know how to do what's fair.

Arnold Palmer

ARNOLD PALMER

Etiquette

CONSIDERATION FOR OTHER PLAYERS

No one should move, talk or stand close to or directly behind the ball or the hole when a player is addressing the ball or making a stroke.

DON'T DELAY

Players should play without delay.

SAFETY FIRST

No player should play until the players in front are out of range.

SEARCHING FOR BALL—PLAYING THROUGH

Players searching for a ball should allow other players coming up to pass them; they should signal to the players following them to pass, and should not continue their play until those players have passed and are out of range.

PRIORITY ON THE COURSE

If a match fails to keep its place on the course and loses more than one clear hole on the players in front, it should invite the match following to pass.

HOLES IN BUNKERS

Before leaving a bunker, a player should carefully fill up and smooth over all holes and footprints made by him.

REPLACE DIVOTS, REPAIR BALL-MARKS AND DAMAGE BY SPIKES

Through the green, a player should ensure that any turf cut or displaced is replaced at once and pressed down and that any damage to the putting green made by a ball is carefully repaired. Damage to the putting green caused by golf shoe spikes should be repaired *on completion of the hole.*

DAMAGE TO GREENS

RIGHT

WRONG

Players should ensure that, when putting down bags or the flagstick, no damage is done to the putting green and that neither they nor their caddies damage the hole by standing close to it, in handling the flagstick or in removing the ball from the hole. The flagstick should be properly replaced in the hole before the players leave the putting green. Players should not damage the putting green by leaning on their putters, particularly when removing the ball from the hole.

Definitions

ADDRESSING THE BALL

A player has "addressed the ball" when he has taken his *stance* and has *also* grounded his club, except that in a *hazard* a player has addressed the ball when he has taken his stance.

ADVICE

"Is my grip right?"

"Is the penalty one or two strokes?"

"Advice" is any counsel or suggestion which could influence a player in determining his play, the choice of a club, or the method of making a *stroke*.

Information on the Rules or on matters of public information, such as the position of hazards or the flagstick on the putting green, is not advice.

BUNKER

SAND
(Hazard)

GREEN

BUNKER

GRASS IN BUNKER
(Not Hazard)

A "bunker" is a *hazard* consisting of a prepared area of ground, often a hollow, from which turf or soil has been removed and replaced with sand or the like. Grass-covered ground bordering or within a bunker is not part of the bunker. The margin of a bunker extends vertically downwards but not upwards.

CASUAL WATER

Not Casual Water

Casual Water

"Casual water" is any temporary accumulation of water on the *course* which is visible before or after the player takes his *stance* and is not in a *water hazard*. Snow and ice are either casual water or *loose impediments,* at the option of the player, except that manufactured ice is an *obstruction*. Dew is not casual water.

GROUND UNDER REPAIR

"Ground under repair" is any portion of the *course* so marked by order of the Committee or so declared by its authorized representative. It includes material piled for removal and a hole made by a greenkeeper, even if not so marked. Stakes and lines defining ground under repair are in such ground. The margin of ground under repair extends vertically downwards, but not upwards.

Note 1: Grass cuttings and other material left on the course which have been abandoned and are not intended to be removed are not ground under repair unless so marked.

Note 2: The Committee may make a Local Rule prohibiting play from ground under repair.

LOOSE IMPEDIMENTS

"Loose impediments" are natural objects such as stones, leaves, twigs, branches and the like, dung, worms and insects and casts or heaps made by them, provided they are not fixed or growing, are not solidly embedded and do not adhere to the ball.

Sand and loose soil are loose impediments on the *putting green,* but not elsewhere.

Snow and ice are either *casual water* or loose impediments, at the option of the player, except that manufactured ice is an *obstruction.*

Dew is not a loose impediment.

LOST BALL

"I've found your first ball!"

"I can't play that one— this one's in play now."

"Here's your original ball."

"Too late. I've just played the provisional from here."

A ball is lost if:

a. It is not found or identified as his by the player within five minutes after the player's side or his or their caddies have begun to search for it; or

b. The player has put another ball into play under the Rules, even though he may not have searched for the original ball; or

c. The player has played any stroke with a *provisional ball* from the place where the original ball is likely to be or from a point nearer the hole than that place, whereupon the provisional ball becomes the *ball in play*.

Time spent in playing a *wrong ball* is not counted in the five-minute period allowed for search.

BALL DEEMED TO MOVE

A ball is deemed to have "moved" if it leaves its position and comes to rest in any other place.

OBSTRUCTIONS

An "obstruction" is anything artificial, including the artificial surfaces and sides of roads and paths and manufactured ice, except:

a. Objects defining *out of bounds,* such as walls, fences, stakes and railings;

b. Any part of an immovable artificial object which is out of bounds; and

c. Any construction declared by the Committee to be an integral part of the course.

OUT OF BOUNDS

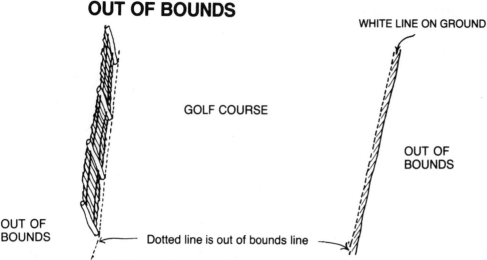

WHITE LINE ON GROUND

GOLF COURSE

OUT OF BOUNDS

OUT OF BOUNDS

Dotted line is out of bounds line

"Out of bounds" is ground on which play is prohibited.

When out of bounds is defined by reference to stakes or a fence or as being beyond stakes or a fence, the out of bounds line is determined by the nearest inside points of the stakes or fence posts at ground level excluding angled supports.

When out of bounds is defined by a line on the ground, the line itself is out of bounds.

The out of bounds line extends vertically upwards and downwards.

A ball is out of bounds when all of it lies out of bounds.

A player may stand out of bounds to play a ball lying within bounds.

OUTSIDE AGENCY— RUB OF THE GREEN

An "outside agency" is any agency not part of the match or, in stroke play, not part of a competitor's side, and includes a referee, a marker, an observer or a forecaddie. Neither wind nor water is an outside agency.

A "rub of the green" occurs when a ball in motion is accidentally deflected or stopped by an *outside agency* (see Rule 19–1).

PARTS OF THE COURSE

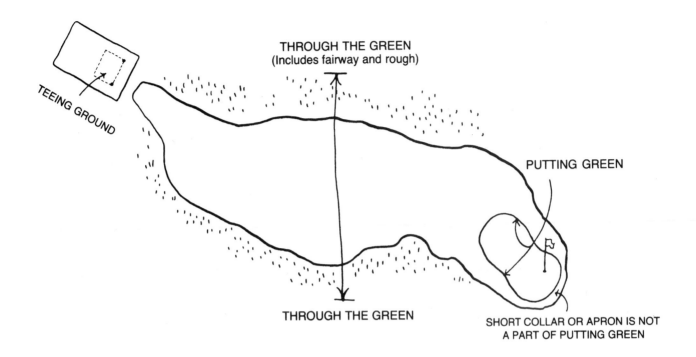

THROUGH THE GREEN
(Includes fairway and rough)

TEEING GROUND

PUTTING GREEN

THROUGH THE GREEN

SHORT COLLAR OR APRON IS NOT
A PART OF PUTTING GREEN

Putting Green

The "putting green" is all ground of the hole being played which is specially prepared for putting or otherwise defined as such by the Committee.

A ball is on the putting green when any part of it touches the putting green.

Teeing Ground

The "teeing ground" is the starting place for the hole to be played. It is a rectangular area two club-lengths in depth, the front and the sides of which are defined by the outside limits of two tee-markers. A ball is outside the teeing ground when all of it lies outside the teeing ground.

Through the Green

"Through the green" is the whole area of the *course* except:

a. The *teeing ground* and *putting green* of the hole being played; and

b. All *hazards* on the course.

SIDES AND MATCHES

Threesome

A threesome is a match in which one plays against two, and each side plays one ball.

Foursome

A foursome is a match in which two play against two, and each side plays one ball.

Three-Ball

A three-ball is a match play competition in which three play against one another, each playing his own ball. Each player is playing two distinct matches.

A best-ball is a match in which one plays against the better ball of two or the best ball of three players.

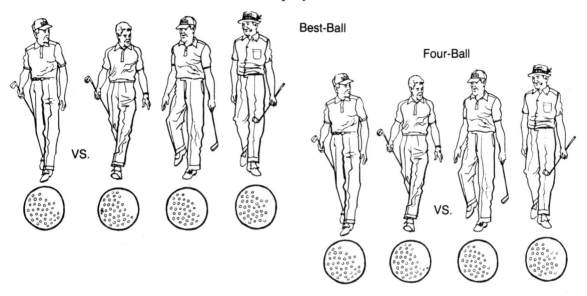

Best-Ball

Four-Ball

VS.

VS.

A four-ball is a match in which two play their better ball against the better ball of two other players.

STROKE

A "stroke" is the forward movement of the club made with the intention of fairly striking at and moving the ball, but if a player checks his downswing voluntarily before the clubhead reaches the ball he is deemed not to have made a stroke.

19

WATER HAZARDS AND LATERAL WATER HAZARDS

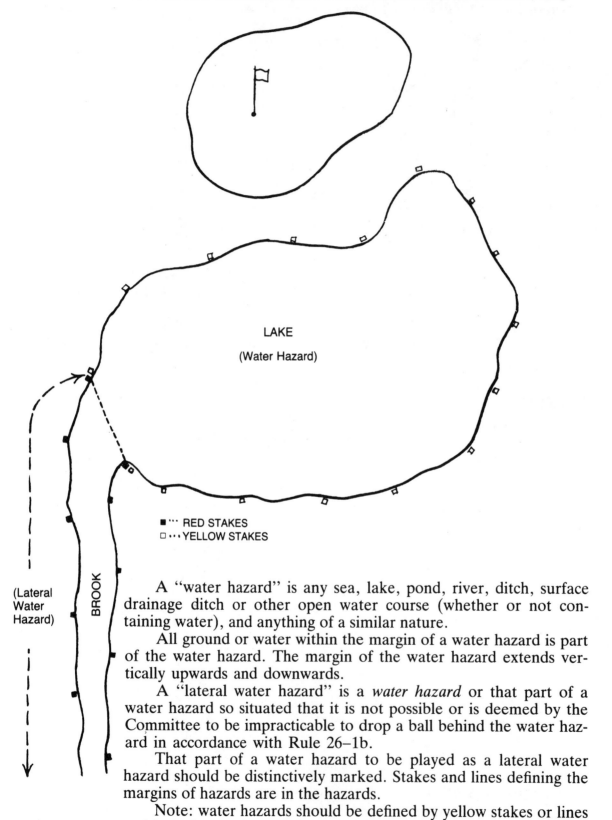

LAKE

(Water Hazard)

■ ··· RED STAKES
□ ··· YELLOW STAKES

(Lateral Water Hazard)

BROOK

A "water hazard" is any sea, lake, pond, river, ditch, surface drainage ditch or other open water course (whether or not containing water), and anything of a similar nature.

All ground or water within the margin of a water hazard is part of the water hazard. The margin of the water hazard extends vertically upwards and downwards.

A "lateral water hazard" is a *water hazard* or that part of a water hazard so situated that it is not possible or is deemed by the Committee to be impracticable to drop a ball behind the water hazard in accordance with Rule 26–1b.

That part of a water hazard to be played as a lateral water hazard should be distinctively marked. Stakes and lines defining the margins of hazards are in the hazards.

Note: water hazards should be defined by yellow stakes or lines and lateral water hazards by red stakes or lines.

The Rules of Play

STIPULATED ROUND; THE GAME

The "stipulated round" consists of playing the holes of the course in their correct sequence unless otherwise authorized by the Committee. The number of holes in a stipulated round is eighteen unless a smaller number is authorized by the Committee.

The Game of Golf consists in playing a ball from the *teeing ground* into the hole by a *stroke* or successive strokes in accordance with the Rules. **Rule 1–1.**

AGREEMENT TO WAIVE RULES

Players shall not agree to exclude the operation of any Rule or to waive any penalty incurred. PENALTY: *Match play—Disqualification of both sides; Stroke play—Disqualification of competitors concerned.* **Rule 1–3.**

MATCH PLAY

DETERMINING A WINNER

9-Hole Match

HOLE	1	2	3	4	5	6	7	8	9	OUT
FRANK	5	5	3	3	4	4	4			
BOBBY	4	4	2	3	4	4	4			

Bobby winner of match 3 up and 2 to play

Holes Won — Holes Halved

Winner of Hole; Reckoning of Holes

In match play the game is played by holes.

Except as otherwise provided in the Rules, a hole is won by the side which holes its ball in the fewer strokes. In a handicap match the lower net score wins the hole.

The reckoning of holes is kept by the terms: so many "holes up" or "all square," and so many "to play."

A side is "dormie" when it is as many holes up as there are holes remaining to be played. **Rule 2-1.**

AN AUTOMATIC HALF

Mr. B is preparing to play his 4th stroke.

Mr. A, who has holed out in 4, says to Mr. B, "Your putt is going to break to the left."

Halved Hole

A hole is halved if each side holes out in the same number of strokes.

When a player has holed out and his opponent has been left with a stroke for the half, if the player thereafter incurs a penalty, the hole is halved. **Rule 2-2.**

Winner of Match

A match (which consists of a *stipulated round,* unless otherwise decreed by the Committee) is won by the side which is leading by a number of holes greater than the number of holes remaining to be played.

The Committe may, for the purpose of settling a tie, extend the stipulated round to as many holes as are required for a match to be won. **Rule 2–3.**

Concession of Next Stroke, Hole or Match

When the opponent's ball is at rest or is deemed to be at rest under Rule 16–2, the player may concede the opponent to have holed out with his next stroke and the ball may be removed by either side with a club or otherwise.

A player may concede a hole or a match at any time prior to the conclusion of the hole or the match.

Concession of a stroke, hole or match may not be declined or withdrawn. **Rule 2–4.**

CLAIMS IN MATCH PLAY

"Did you break a Rule on the last hole when you dropped away from that fence?"

Claims

In match play, if a doubt or dispute arises between the players and no duly authorized representative of the Committee is available within a reasonable time, the players shall continue the match without delay. Any claim, if it is to be considered by the Committee, must be made before any player in the match plays from the next teeing ground or, in the case of the last hole of the match, before all players in the match leave the putting green.

No later claim shall be considered unless it is based on facts previously unknown to the player making the claim and the player making the claim had been given wrong information (Rules 6–2a and 9) by an opponent. In any case, no later claim shall be considered after the result of the match has been officially announced, unless the Committee is satisfied that the opponent knew he was giving wrong information. **Rule 2–5.**

STROKE PLAY

DETERMINING A WINNER

HOLE	OUT	10	11	12	13	14	15	16	17	18	IN	TOTAL
FRANK	38	5	3	3	4	5	4	3	4	5	36	74
BOBBY	35	5	4	4	4	5	5	3	4	3	37	72

Bobby is the winner

The competitor who plays the *stipulated round* or rounds in the fewest strokes is the winner. **Rule 3–1.**

FAILURE TO HOLE OUT

"This is a gimme."

"No! This is stroke play. You must hole out."

If a competitor fails to hole out at any hole and does not correct his mistake before he plays a *stroke* from the next *teeing ground,* or, in the case of the last hole of the round, before he leaves the *putting green, he shall be disqualified.* **Rule 3–2.**

DOUBT AS TO PROCEDURE

a. Procedure

In stroke play only, when during play of a hole a competitor is doubtful of his rights or procedure, he may, without penalty, play a second ball. After the situation which caused the doubt has arisen, the competitor should, before taking further action, announce to his marker or a fellow-competitor his decision to invoke this Rule and the ball with which he will score if the Rules permit.

The competitor shall report the facts to the *Committee* before returning his score card unless he scores the same with both balls; if he fails to do so, *he shall be disqualified.*

b. Determination of Score for Hole

If the Rules allow the procedure selected in advance by the competitor, the score with the ball selected shall be his score for the hole.

If the competitor fails to announce in advance his decision to invoke this Rule or his selection, the score with the original ball or, if the original ball is not one of the balls being played, the first ball put into play shall count if the Rules allow the procedure adopted for such ball. **Rule 3–3.**

"I think this should be ground under repair. I'll play this ball as it lies, and a second ball under Rule 3–3. I want to score with the second ball."

GENERAL PENALTY

"There's no penalty given for breaking that Local Rule."

Except when otherwise provided for, the PENALTY for a breach of a Rule is: *Match play—Loss of hole; Stroke play—Two strokes.* **Rules 2–6 and 3–5.**

THE CLUB

Movable Parts Prohibited

The club shall be composed of a shaft and a head. All parts of the club shall be fixed so that the club is one unit. The club shall not be designed to be adjustable except for weight. The club shall not be substantially different from the traditional and customary form and make. **Rule 4–1a.**

THE GRIP

CLUB GRIP CIRCULAR

PUTTER GRIP FLAT SIDE (Permitted on Putters only)

The grip consists of that part of the shaft designed to be held by the player and any material added to it for the purpose of obtaining a firm hold. The grip shall be substantially straight and plain in form and shall not be molded for any part of the hands. Except for putters, the grip must be generally circular in cross-section. A putter grip may have a non-circular cross-section, provided the cross-section has no concavity. **Rule 4–1c and App. II.**

MAXIMUM OF FOURTEEN CLUBS

"Let's be sure I have only fourteen clubs."

Selection and Replacement of Clubs

The player shall start a *stipulated round* with not more than fourteen clubs. He is limited to the clubs thus selected for that round except that, without unduly delaying play, he may:

(i) if he started with fewer than fourteen, add as many as will bring his total to that number; and

(ii) replace, with any club, a club which becomes unfit for play in the normal course of play.

Borrowing or Sharing Clubs

The addition or replacement of a club or clubs may be made by borrowing from anyone; only the borrower may use such club or clubs for the remainder of the round.

The sharing of a club or clubs is prohibited except that partners may share clubs, provided that the total number of clubs carried by the partners so sharing does not exceed fourteen.

PENALTY: *Match play—At the conclusion of the hole at which the breach is discovered, the state of the match shall be adjusted by deducting one hole for each hole at which a breach occurred. Maximum deduction per round: two holes. Stroke play—Two strokes for each hole at which any breach occurred; maximum penalty per round: four strokes.* **Rules 4–4a and 4–4b.**

Excess Club Declared Out of Play

Any club carried or used in breach of this Rule shall be declared out of play by the player immediately upon discovery that a breach has occurred and thereafter shall not be used by the player during the round. PENALTY: *Disqualification.* **Rule 4–4c.**

THE BALL

"Isn't that a small ball you're using?"

"Yes—but I use it only once in a while."

The weight of the ball shall *not* be *greater* than 1.620 ounces avoirdupois, and the size *not less* than 1.680 inches in diameter.
PENALTY: *Disqualification.* **Appendix III a and b.**

BALL UNFIT FOR PLAY

A ball is unfit for play if it is visibly cut, cracked or out of shape. A ball is not unfit for play solely because mud or other materials adhere to it, its surface is scratched or scraped or its paint is damaged or discolored.

If a player has reason to believe his ball has become unfit for play during play of the hole being played, he may during the play of such hole lift his ball without penalty to determine whether it is unfit, provided he announces his intention in advance to his opponent in match play or his marker or a fellow-competitor in stroke play and gives his opponent, marker or fellow-competitor an opportunity to examine the ball. If he lifts the ball without announcing his intention in advance or giving his opponent, marker or fellow-competitor an opportunity to examine the ball, *he shall incur a PENALTY of one stroke.* **Rule 5–3.**

"I'm going to play this cut ball on this water hole."

"Then you can't change the ball on the green."

If it is determined that the ball has become unfit for play during play of the hole being played, the player may substitute another ball, placing it on the spot where the original ball lay. Otherwise, the original ball shall be replaced.

If a ball breaks into pieces as a result of a stroke, the stroke shall be replayed without penalty (see Rule 20–5). *PENALTY for breach of Rule 5–3: *Match play—Loss of hole; Stroke play—Two strokes.*

*If a player incurs the general penalty for breach of Rule 5–3, no additional penalty under the Rule shall be applied.

Note 1: The ball may not be cleaned to determine whether it is unfit for play—See Rule 21.

Note 2: If the opponent, marker or fellow-competitor wishes to dispute a claim of unfitness, he must do so before the player plays another ball.

PLAYER'S RESPONSIBILITIES

CONDITIONS OF COMPETITION

The player is responsible for knowing the conditions under which the competition is to be played. **Rule 6–1.**

CHECKING HANDICAP

Match Play

Before starting a match in a handicap competition, the players should determine from one another their respective handicaps. If a player begins the match having declared a higher handicap which would affect the number of strokes given or received, *he shall be disqualified;* otherwise, the player shall play off the declared handicap. **Rule 6–2a.**

Stroke Play

In any round of a handicap competition, the competitor shall ensure that his handicap is recorded on his score card before it is returned to the Committee. If no handicap is recorded on his score card before it is returned, or if the recorded handicap is higher than that to which he is entitled and this affects the number of strokes received, *he shall be disqualified* from that round of the handicap competition; otherwise, the score shall stand. **Rule 6–2b.**

Note: It is the player's responsibility to know the holes at which handicap strokes are to be given or received.

BREACH OF RULE BY CADDIE

"You can't do that!"

"Those last fellows certainly scuffed up the green."

For any breach of a Rule by his caddie, the player incurs the applicable penalty. **Rule 6–4.**

IDENTIFICATION MARK ON BALL

The responsibility for playing the proper ball rests with the player. Each player should put an identification mark on his ball. **Rule 6–5.**

SIGNING AND RETURNING CARD

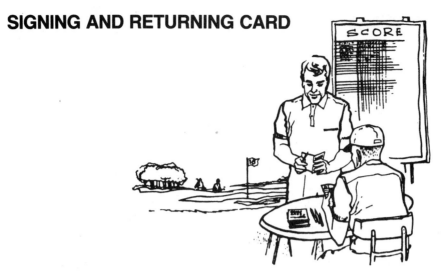

After completion of the round, the competitor should check his score for each hole and settle any doubtful points with the Committee. He shall ensure that the marker has signed the card, countersign the card himself and return it to the Committee as soon as possible. **Rule 6–6b.**

PENALTY for breach of Rule 6–6b: *Disqualification.*

NO ALTERATION OF CARD; WRONG SCORE FOR HOLE

"May I see that card I turned in about an hour ago? I think I put down a 5 for the 18th, but I actually had a 6."

No alteration may be made on a card after the competitor has returned it to the Committee. **Rule 6–6c.**

The competitor is responsible for the correctness of the score recorded for each hole. If he returns a score for any hole lower than actually taken, *he shall be disqualified.*

If he returns a score for any hole higher than actually taken, the score as returned shall stand. **Rule 6–6d.**

Note 1: The Committee is responsible for the addition of scores and application of the handicap recorded on the card—see Rule 33–5.

Note 2: In four-ball stroke play, see also Rules 31–4 and 7a.

UNDUE DELAY

The player shall play without undue delay. Between completion of a hole and playing from the next tee, the player shall not unduly delay play. **Rule 6–7.** PENALTY for breach of Rule: *Match play—Loss of hole; Stroke play—Two strokes. For repeated offense—Disqualification.*

If the player delays play between holes, he is delaying the play of the next hole, and the penalty applies to that hole.

DISCONTINUANCE OF PLAY

The player shall not discontinue play unless:
(i) the Committee has suspended play;
(ii) he believes there is danger from lightning;
(iii) he is seeking a decision from the Committee on a doubtful or disputed point (see Rules 2–5 and 34–3); or
(iv) there is some other good reason such as sudden illness.
Bad weather is not of itself a good reason for discontinuing play.

If the player discontinues play without specific permission from the Committee, he shall report to the Committee as soon as practicable. If he does so and the Committee considers his reason satisfactory, the player incurs no penalty. Otherwise, *the player shall be disqualified.* **Rule 6–8a.**

Exception in match play: Players discontinuing match play by agreement are not subject to disqualification unless by so doing the competition is delayed.

Note: Leaving the course does not of itself constitute discontinuance of play.

PRACTICE

BEFORE OR BETWEEN ROUNDS

1st hole

Match Play

On any day of a match play competition, a player may practice on the competition *course* before a round. **Rule 7–1a.**

Stroke Play

On any day of a stroke competition or play-off, a competitor shall not practice on the competition *course* or test the surface of any putting green on the course before a round or play-off. When two or more rounds of a stroke competition are to be played over consecutive days, practice between those rounds on any competition course remaining to be played is prohibited. PENALTY: *Disqualification.* **Rule 7–1b.**

Exception: Practice putting or chipping on or near the first *teeing ground* before starting a round or play-off is permitted.

DURING ROUND

"Watch out, Hank; I'm playing another shot for practice."

During Play of Hole

"As long as we have to wait, don't you think it would be all right if we tried a few practice putts on the 9th green?"

"Can't do it—it's against the Rules."

Between Holes

A player shall not play a practice *stroke* either during the play of a hole or between the play of two holes except that, between the play of two holes, the player may practice putting or chipping on or near the *putting green* of the hole last played, any practice putting green or the *teeing ground* of the next hole to be played in the round, provided such practice stroke is not played from a hazard and does not unduly delay play. **Rule 7–2.** PENALTY for breach of Rule 7-2: *Match play—Loss of hole; Stroke play—Two strokes.*

In the event of a breach between the play of two holes, the penalty applies to the next hole.

Note: A practice swing is not a practice *stroke* and may be taken at any place, provided the player does not breach the Rules.

ADVICE; INDICATING LINE OF PLAY

GIVING OR ASKING FOR ADVICE

"Fine shot. What club did you use?"

A player shall not give advice to anyone in the competition except his partner. A player may ask for advice from only his partner or either of their caddies. **Rule 8–1.**

INDICATING LINE OF PLAY

"Your line is straight over the bag."

"That's against the Rules. Take the bag away, please."

Other Than on Putting Green

Except on the *putting green,* a player may have the line of play indicated to him by anyone, but no one shall stand on or close to the line while the *stroke* is being played. Any mark placed during the play of a hole by the player or with his knowledge to indicate the line shall be removed before the stroke is played. **Rule 8–2a.**

Exception: Flagstick attended or held up—Rule 17–1.

On the Putting Green

When the player's ball is on the *putting green,* the player, his partner or either of their caddies may, before but not during the *stroke,* point out a line for putting, but in so doing the putting green shall not be touched. No mark shall be placed anywhere to indicate a line for putting. **Rule 8–2b.** PENALTY for breach of rule: *Match play—Loss of hole; Stroke play—Two strokes.*

WRONG

"Putt it for here."

Club touching green

RIGHT

Club held off green

INFORMATION AS TO STROKES TAKEN

"I lie 5, and not 4 as I said before you played your last shot. I forgot to include a penalty on my second shot. Sorry."

General

The number of strokes a player has taken shall include any penalty strokes incurred. **Rule 9–1.**

Match Play

A player who has incurred a penalty shall inform his opponent as soon as practicable. If he fails to do so, he shall be deemed to have given wrong information, even if he was not aware that he had incurred a penalty.

An opponent is entitled to ascertain from the player, during the play of a hole, the number of strokes he has taken and, after play of a hole, the number of strokes taken on the hole just completed.

If during the play of a hole the player gives or is deemed to give wrong information as to the number of strokes taken, he shall incur no penalty if he corrects the mistake before his opponent has played his next stroke. If the player fails so to correct the wrong information, *he shall lose the hole.*

If after play of a hole the player gives or is deemed to give wrong information as to the number of strokes taken on the hole just completed and this affects the opponent's understanding of the result of the hole, he shall incur no penalty if he corrects his mistake before any player plays from the next *teeing ground* or, in the case of the last hole of the match, before all players leave the *putting green.* If the player fails so to correct the wrong information, *he shall lose the hole.* **Rule 9–2.**

ORDER OF PLAY

TEEING GROUND AND OTHER THAN ON TEEING GROUND

Match Play and Stroke Play

On the teeing ground, the side with the honor shall play first. Other than on the teeing ground, the ball farther from the hole shall be played first. If two balls are equidistant from the hole, the ball to be played first should be decided by lot. **Rules 10–1a and 1b and 10–2a and 2b.**

Exceptions: Rule 30–3c (best-ball and four-ball match play).
Rule 22 (ball interfering with or assisting play).
Rule 31–5 (four-ball stroke play).

PLAYING OUT OF TURN

"I believe it was my honor."

Match Play

If a player plays when his opponent should have played, the opponent may immediately require the player to cancel the stroke so played and play a ball in correct order, without penalty. **Rule 10–1c** (see also Rule 20–5).

Stroke Play

If a competitor plays out of turn, no penalty shall be incurred and the ball shall be played as it lies. If, however, the Committee determines that competitors have agreed to play in an order other than that set forth in Clauses 2a and 2b of this Rule to give one of them an advantage, *they shall be disqualified.* **Rule 10–2c.**

SECOND BALL FROM TEEING GROUND

Who drives next?

Out of Bounds

If a player plays a *provisional ball* or a second ball from a *teeing ground,* he should do so after his opponent or fellow-competitor has played his first *stroke.* If a player plays a provisional ball or a second ball out of turn, Clauses 1c and 2c of this Rule shall apply. **Rule 10–3.**

TEEING GROUND

BALL FALLING OFF TEE

If a ball, when not in *play,* falls off a tee or is knocked off a tee by the player in addressing it, it may be re-teed without penalty, but if a *stroke* is made at the ball in these circumstances, whether the ball is moving or not, the stroke counts but no penalty is incurred. **Rule 11–3.**

PLAYING OUTSIDE TEEING GROUND

Stance legal

Ball's position wrong

Match Play

If a player, when starting a hole, plays a ball from outside the *teeing ground,* the opponent may immediately require the player to cancel the stroke so played and play a ball from within the teeing ground, without penalty. **Rule 11–4a.**

Stroke Play

If a competitor, when starting a hole, plays a ball from outside the *teeing ground, he shall incur a penalty of two strokes* and shall then play a ball from within the teeing ground.

If the competitor plays a stroke from the next teeing ground without first correcting his mistake or, in the case of the last hole of the round, leaves the *putting green* without first declaring his intention to correct his mistake, *he shall be disqualified.*

Strokes played by a competitor from outside the teeing ground do not count in his score. **Rule 11–4b.**

Teeing; Tee-Markers

A player may stand outside the *teeing ground* to play a ball within it.

Before a player plays his first stroke with any ball from the teeing ground of the hole being played, the tee-markers are deemed to be fixed. **Rules 11–1 and 11–2.**

SEARCHING FOR BALL;
IDENTIFYING BALL

SEEING BALL

Are you always allowed to see
the ball when you play?

In searching for his ball anywhere on the course, the player
may touch or bend long grass, rushes, bushes, whins, heather or the
like, but only to the extent necessary to find and identify it, provided that this does not improve the lie of the ball, the area of his
intended swing or his line of play. **Rule 12–1.**

SEARCHING FOR BALL

*"I'm sure the ball is
here someplace."*

*"My ball must be
buried in the sand."*

In a *hazard,* if a ball is covered by *loose impediments* or sand,
the player may remove by probing, raking or other means as much
thereof as will enable him to see a part of the ball. If an excess is
removed, no penalty is incurred and the ball shall be re-covered so
that only a part of the ball is visible. If the ball is moved in such
removal, no penalty is incurred; the ball shall be replaced and, if
necessary, re-covered. As to removal of loose impediments outside
a hazard, see Rule 23.

If a ball lying in *casual water, ground under repair* or a hole, cast or runway made by a burrowing animal, a reptile or a bird is accidentally moved during search, no penalty is incurred; the ball shall be replaced, unless the player elects to proceed under Rule 25–1b.

If a ball is believed to be lying in water in a *water hazard,* the player may probe for it with a club or otherwise. If the ball is moved in so doing, no penalty is incurred; the ball shall be replaced, unless the player elects to proceed under Rule 26–1. (Continuation of **Rule 12–1**). PENALTY for breach of Rule 12–1: *Match play—Loss of hole; Stroke play—Two strokes.*

IDENTIFYING BALL

May he lift the ball?

Yes · No · Sand in bunker

Except in a *hazard,* the player may, without penalty, lift a ball he believes to be his own for the purpose of identification and clean it to the extent necessary for identification. If the ball is the player's ball, he shall replace it. Before the player lifts the ball, he shall announce his intention to his opponent in match play or his marker or a fellow-competitor in stroke play and give his opponent, marker or fellow-competitor an opportunity to observe the lifting and replacement. If he lifts his ball without announcing his intention in advance or giving his opponent, marker or fellow-competitor an opportunity to observe, or if he lifts his ball for identification in a hazard, *he shall incur a penalty of one stroke* and the ball shall be replaced. **Rule 12–2.**

BALL PLAYED AS IT LIES; AREA OF INTENDED SWING AND LINE OF PLAY; STANCE

BALL PLAYED AS IT LIES

The ball shall be played as it lies except as otherwise provided in the Rules. **Rule 13–1.** (Ball at rest moved, see Rule 18.)

IMPROVING LIE, AREA OF INTENDED SWING OR LINE OF PLAY

Except as provided in the Rules, a player shall not improve or allow to be improved:
the position or lie of his ball,
the area of his intended swing,
his line of play or
the area in which he is to drop or place a ball
by any of the following actions:
moving, bending or breaking anything growing or fixed (including immovable obstructions and objects defining *out of bounds*) or
removing or pressing down sand, loose soil, replaced divots, other cut turf placed in position or other irregularities of surface except as follows:
as may occur in fairly taking his *stance,*
in making a *stroke* or the backward movement of his club for a stroke,
on the *teeing ground* in creating or eliminating irregularities of surface, or
on the *putting green* in removing sand and loose soil as provided in Rule 16–1a or in repairing damage as provided in Rule 16–1c.

"Do you want me to hold back this limb?"

How hard may the player press down the grass?

The club may be grounded only lightly and shall not be pressed on the ground. **Rule 13–2.**

Exception: Ball lying in or touching hazard (Rule 13–4).

BUILDING STANCE

This is wrong

A player is entitled to place his feet firmly in taking his stance, but he shall not build a stance. **Rule 13–3.**

BALL LYING IN OR TOUCHING HAZARD

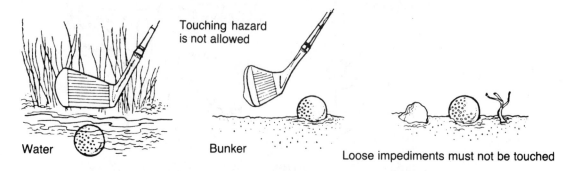

Touching hazard is not allowed

Water

Bunker

Loose impediments must not be touched

Except as provided in the Rules, before making a *stroke* at a ball which lies in or touches a *hazard* (whether a *bunker* or a *water hazard*), the player shall not:

a. Test the condition of the hazard or any similar hazard,

b. Touch the ground in the hazard or water in the water hazard with a club or otherwise, or

c. Touch or move a *loose impediment* lying in or touching the hazard.

Exceptions:

1. At address or in the backward movement for the stroke, the club may touch any obstruction or any grass, bush, tree or other growing thing.

2. The player may place his clubs in a *hazard,* provided nothing is done which may constitute testing the soil or improving the lie of the ball.

3. The player after playing the stroke, or his *caddie* at any time without the authority of the player, may smooth sand or soil in the hazard, provided that, if the ball still lies in the hazard, nothing is done which improves the lie of the ball or assists the player in his subsequent play of the hole. **Rule 13–4.** PENALTY for breach of Rule: *Match play—Loss of hole; Stroke play—Two strokes.*

Smoothing Irregularities

Bunker

STRIKING THE BALL

BALL TO BE FAIRLY STRUCK AT

WRONG

The ball shall be fairly struck at with the head of a club and must not be pushed, scraped or spooned. **Rule 14–1.**

ASSISTANCE

In making a stroke a player shall not accept physical assistance or protection from the elements. **Rule 14–2.** PENALTY for breach of Rule 14–1 or –2: *Match play—Loss of hole; Stroke play—Two strokes.*

ARTIFICIAL DEVICES AND UNUSUAL EQUIPMENT

Except as provided in the Rules, during a stipulated round the player shall not use any artificial device or unusual equipment:

a. For the purpose of gauging or measuring distance or conditions which might affect his play; or

b. Which might assist him in gripping the club, in making a stroke or in his play, except that plain gloves may be worn, resin, tape or gauze may be applied to the grip (provided such application does not render the grip nonconforming under Rule 4–1c), and a towel or handkerchief may be wrapped around the grip. **Rule 14–3.**
PENALTY for breach of Rule 14–3: *Disqualification.*

STRIKING BALL MORE THAN ONCE

If a player's club strikes the ball more than once in the course of a *stroke,* the player shall count the stroke and *add a penalty stroke,* making two strokes in all. **Rule 14–4.**

PLAYING MOVING BALL

Playing a moving ball is prohibited . . .   . . . but . . .

IN
WATER HAZARD

A player shall not play while his ball is moving. **Rule 14–5.**
Exceptions:
Ball falling off tee—**Rule 11–3.**
Striking the ball more than once—**Rule 14–4.**
Ball moving in water—**Rule 14–6.**
When the ball begins to move only after the player has begun the *stroke* or the backward movement of his club for the stroke, he shall incur no penalty under this Rule for playing a moving ball, but he is not exempt from any penalty incurred under the following Rules:
Ball at rest moved by player—**Rule 18–2a.**
Ball at rest moving after address—**Rule 18–2b.**
Ball at rest moving after loose impediment touched—**Rule 18–2c.**

Ball Moving in Water

When a ball is moving in water in a *water hazard*, the player may, without penalty, make a *stroke*, but he must not delay making his stroke in order to allow the wind or current to improve the position of the ball. A ball moving in water in a water hazard may be lifted if the player elects to invoke Rule 26. **Rule 14–6.** PENALTY for breach of Rule 14–5 or –6: *Match play—Loss of hole; Stroke play—Two strokes.*

PLAYING A WRONG BALL

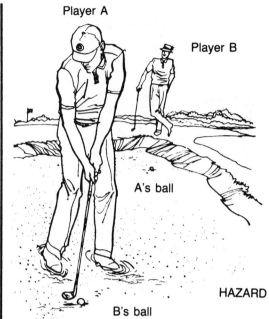

General

A player must hole out with the ball played from the *teeing ground* unless a Rule permits him to substitute another ball. **Rule 15–1.**

Match Play

If a player plays a stroke with a *wrong ball*, except in a *hazard, he shall lose the hole.* When the player and the opponent exchange balls during the play of a hole, the first to play the wrong ball other than from a hazard shall lose the hole; when this cannot be determined, the hole shall be played out with the balls exchanged. **Rule 15–2.**

Stroke Play

If the competitor plays a stroke with the wrong ball except in a hazard, *he shall add two penalty strokes to his score* for the hole and shall then play the correct ball (provided he has not made a stroke on the next teeing ground, or, in the case of the last hole of the round, has not left the putting green). Strokes played with a wrong ball do not count in his score. **Rule 15–3.**

There is no penalty for a player playing a stroke or strokes in a hazard with a wrong ball provided he then plays the correct ball, in match play and stroke play. Strokes played with a wrong ball do not count in his score. **Rule 15–2, –3.**

THE PUTTING GREEN

TOUCHING LINE OF PUTT

The line of putt must not be touched except:

(i) the player may move sand and loose soil on the putting green and other *loose impediments* by picking them up or by brushing them aside with his hand or a club without pressing anything down;

(ii) in addressing the ball, the player may place the club in front of the ball without pressing anything down;

(iii) in measuring—**Rule 10–4**;

(iv) in lifting the ball—**Rule 16–1b**;

(v) in pressing down a ball-marker;

(vi) in repairing old hole plugs or ball marks on the putting green—**Rule 16–1c**; and

(vii) in removing movable *obstructions*—**Rule 24–1.**

(Indicating line for putting on putting green—see Rule 8–2b.)

BALL

club may be placed in front of ball without pressing anything down

TWIG

loose impediment may be removed

may be repaired

BALL MARK

HOLE

may not be repaired

SPIKE MARKS

STANDING ASTRIDE OR ON LINE OF PUTT

The player shall not make a *stroke* on the *putting green* from a *stance* astride, or with either foot touching, the line of the putt or an extension of that line behind the ball. For the purpose of this Clause only, the line of putt does not extend beyond the hole. **Rule 16–1e.**

POSITION OF CADDIE OR PARTNER

While making the *stroke,* the player shall not allow his caddie, his partner or his partner's caddie to position himself on or close to an extension of the line of putt behind the ball. **Rule 16–1f.**

PLAYING STROKE WHILE ANOTHER BALL IN MOTION

A player shall not play a stroke while another ball is in motion after a stroke on the putting green. **Rule 16–1g.**

BALL OVERHANGING HOLE

When any part of the ball overhangs the lip of the hole, the player is allowed enough time to reach the hole without unreasonable delay and an additional ten seconds to determine whether the ball is at rest. If by then the ball has not fallen into the hole, it is deemed to be at rest. If the ball subsequently falls into the hole, the player is deemed to have holed out with his last stroke, and *he shall add a penalty stroke to his score* for the hole; otherwise there is no penalty under this Rule. **Rule 16–2.**

(Undue delay—see Rule 6–7.)

THE FLAGSTICK

ATTENDED, REMOVED OR HELD UP

Before and during the *stroke,* the player may have the flagstick attended, removed or held up to indicate the position of the hole. This may be done only on the authority of the player before he plays his stroke.

If the flagstick is attended, removed or held up by an opponent, a fellow-competitor or the caddie of either with the player's knowledge and no objection is made, the player shall be deemed to have authorized it. **Rule 17–1.**

WHEN DEEMED ATTENDED

ATTENDED   ATTENDED   NOT ATTENDED

If a player or a caddie attends, removes or holds up the flagstick or stands near the hole while a stroke is being played, he shall be deemed to be attending the flagstick until the ball comes to rest.

If the flagstick is not attended before the stroke is played, it shall not be attended or removed while the ball is in motion. **Rule 17–1.**

BALL STRIKING FLAGSTICK OR ATTENDANT

Flagstick Unattended;
Play off Green

Flagstick Attended;
Play from or off Green

The player's ball shall not strike:

a. The flagstick when attended, removed or held up by the player, his partner or either of their caddies, or by another person with the player's knowledge or authority; or

b. The player's caddie, his partner or his partner's caddie when attending the flagstick, or another person attending the flagstick with the player's knowledge or authority, or *equipment* carried by any such person; or

53

c. The flagstick in the hole, unattended, when the ball has been played from the *putting green*. **Rule 17–3.** PENALTY for breach of Rule: *Match play—Loss of hole; Stroke play—Two strokes, and the ball shall be played as it lies.*

BALL RESTING AGAINST FLAGSTICK

If the ball rests against the flagstick when it is in the hole, the player or another person authorized by him may move or remove the flagstick and if the ball falls into the hole, the player shall be deemed to have holed out at his last stroke; otherwise, the ball, if *moved*, shall be placed on the lip of the hole, without penalty. **Rule 17–4.**

BALL MOVED OR DEFLECTED

BY OUTSIDE AGENCY

"Drop that ball."

If a ball at rest is moved by an *outside agency,* the player shall incur no penalty and the ball shall be replaced before the player plays another *stroke.* **Rule 18–1.**

BY PLAYER, PARTNER, CADDIE

When a player's ball is *in play,* if (i) the player, his partner or either of their caddies lifts or moves it, touches it purposely (except with a club in the act of addressing it) or causes it to move except as permitted by a Rule, or (ii) equipment of the player or his partner causes the ball to move, *the player shall incur a penalty stroke.* The ball shall be replaced unless the movement of the ball occurs after the player has begun his swing and he does not discontinue his swing. **Rule 18–2a.**

"Gosh, Mr. A—
I moved your ball.
That's a penalty."

Caddie A

A's ball

"You shouldn't have lifted my ball out of the divot."

BALL MOVING AFTER ADDRESS

If a player's *ball in play moves* after he has addressed it (other than as a result of a stroke), the player shall be deemed to have moved the ball and *shall incur a penalty stroke.* The player shall replace the ball unless the movement of the ball occurs after he has begun his swing and he does not discontinue his swing. **Rule 18–2b.**

BALL MOVED BY OPPONENT'S OR FELLOW-COMPETITOR'S SIDE DURING SEARCH

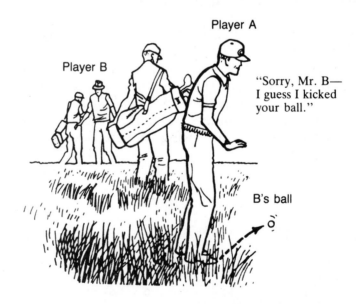

Match Play

If, during search for a player's ball, it is moved by an opponent, his caddie or his *equipment,* no penalty is incurred and the player shall replace the ball. **Rule 18–3a.**

Stroke Play

If a competitor's ball is moved by a fellow-competitor, his caddie or his *equipment*, no penalty is incurred. The competitor shall replace his ball. **Rule 18–4.**

BALL MOVED OTHER THAN DURING SEARCH

Match Play

If, other than during search for a ball, the ball is touched or moved by an opponent, his caddie or his *equipment*, except as otherwise provided in the Rules, *the opponent shall incur a penalty stroke.* The player shall replace the ball. **Rule 18–3b.**

"Hey, you kicked my ball."

Player B

Player A

B's ball

Stroke Play

If a competitor's ball is moved by a fellow-competitor, his caddie or his *equipment*, no penalty is incurred. The competitor shall replace his ball. **Rule 18–4.**

BALL MOVED BY ANOTHER BALL

Player A

Player B

A's ball
moves B's ball

A's ball

B's ball

If a ball in play and at rest is moved by another ball in motion after a stroke, the moved ball shall be replaced. **Rule 18–5.** *PENALTY for breach of Rule: *Match play—Loss of hole; Stroke play—Two strokes.*

*If a player who is required to replace a ball fails to do so, he shall incur the general penalty for breach of Rule 18 but no additional penalty under Rule 18 shall be applied.

Note 1: If a ball to be replaced under this Rule is not immediately recoverable, another ball may be substituted.

Note 2: If it is impossible to determine the spot on which a ball is to be placed, see Rule 20–3c.

BALL IN MOTION DEFLECTED OR STOPPED

By Outside Agency

If a ball in motion is accidentally deflected or stopped by any *outside agency,* it is a *rub of the green,* no penalty is incurred, and the ball shall be played as it lies, except:

1. Outside agency
   No penalty

2. Match play
   Player's own caddie
   Player loses hole

3. Match play
   Opponent's caddie,
   accidentally
   No penalty. Player has
   option to replay

4. Stroke play
   Player's own caddie
   Two-stroke penalty

5. Stroke play
   Fellow-competitor's
   caddie
   No penalty, but
   see Rule for exceptions

a. If a ball in motion after a *stroke* other than on the *putting green* comes to rest in or on any moving or animate outside agency, the player shall, *through the green* or in a *hazard,* drop the ball, or on the putting green place the ball, as near as possible to the spot where the outside agency was when the ball came to rest in or on it; and

b. If a ball in motion after a stroke on the putting green is deflected or stopped by, or comes to rest in or on, any moving or animate outside agency, except a worm or an insect, the stroke shall be canceled and the ball shall be replaced.

If the ball is not immediately recoverable, another ball may be substituted. **Rule 19–1.**

By Player—Match Play

If a player's ball is accidentally deflected or stopped by himself, his partner or either of their caddies or *equipment, he shall lose the hole.* **Rule 19–2a.**

By Competitor—Stroke Play

If a competitor's ball is accidentally deflected or stopped by himself, his partner or either of their caddies or *equipment, the competitor shall incur a PENALTY of two strokes.*

By Opponent, Accidentally—Match Play

If a player's ball is accidentally deflected or stopped by an opponent, his caddie or *equipment,* no penalty is incurred. The player may play the ball as it lies or, before another *stroke* is played by either side, cancel the stroke and replay the stroke (see Rule 20–5). **Rule 19–3.**

Exception: Ball striking person attending a flagstick—see Rule 17-3b.

(Ball purposely deflected or stopped by opponent or caddie—see Rule 1-2.)

BALL DEFLECTED BY ANOTHER BALL

If a player's ball in motion after a stroke is deflected or stopped by a ball at rest, the player shall play his ball as it lies. In stroke play, if both balls lay on the *putting green* prior to the stroke, *the player incurs a penalty of two strokes.* Otherwise, no penalty is incurred.

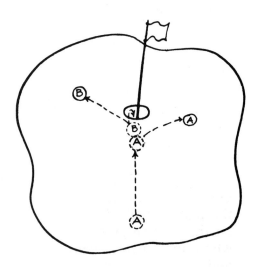

If a player's ball in motion after a stroke is deflected or stopped by another ball in motion, the player shall play his ball as it lies. There is no penalty unless the player was in breach of Rule 16–1g, in which case *he shall incur the penalty for breach of that Rule.* **Rule 19–5.**

Exception: Ball in motion after a stroke on the putting green deflected or stopped by moving or animate outside agency—see Rule 19–1b.

PENALTY for breach of Rule:
Match play—Loss of hole; Stroke play—Two strokes.

LIFTING, DROPPING AND PLACING; PLAYING FROM A WRONG PLACE

LIFTING

Player A

B's ball

Player B   A's ball

A ball to be lifted under the Rules may be lifted by the player, his partner or another person authorized by the player. In any such case, the player shall be responsible for any breach of the Rules.

BALL TO BE MARKED WHEN LIFTED

The position of the ball shall be marked before it is lifted under a Rule which requires it to be replaced. If it is not marked, the player *shall incur a penalty of one stroke* and the ball shall be replaced. If it is not replaced, the *player shall incur the general penalty* for breach of this Rule but no additional penalty under Rule 20–1 shall be applied.

If a ball or a ball-marker is accidentally moved in the process of lifting the ball under a Rule or marking its position, no penalty is incurred and the ball or the ball-marker shall be replaced.

Note: The position of a ball to be lifted should be marked by placing a ball-marker, a small coin or other similar object immediately behind the ball. If the ball-marker interferes with the play, *stance* or *stroke* of another player, it should be placed one or more clubhead-lengths to one side. **Rule 20–1.**

DROPPING AND RE-DROPPING

By Whom and How

A ball to be dropped under the Rules shall be dropped by the player himself. He shall stand erect, hold the ball at shoulder height and arm's length and drop it. If a ball is dropped by any other person or in any other manner and the error is not corrected as provided in Rule 20–6, *the player shall incur a penalty stroke.*

If the ball touches the player, his partner, either of their caddies or their equipment before or after it strikes the ground, the ball shall be re-dropped, without penalty. There is no limit to the number of times a ball shall be re-dropped in such circumstances. **Rule 20–2a.**

WHERE TO DROP

When a ball is to be dropped, it shall be dropped as near as possible to the spot where the ball lay, but not nearer the hole, except when a Rule permits or requires it to be dropped elsewhere. If a ball is to be dropped in a *hazard,* the ball shall be dropped in and come to rest in that hazard. **Rule 20–2b.**

DROPPED BALL ROLLING INTO NEW SITUATION

Water hazard

A dropped ball shall be re-dropped without penalty if it rolls (i) into a *hazard;* (ii) out of a hazard; (iii) onto a *putting green;* (iv) *out of bounds;* (v) back into the condition from which relief was taken under Rule 24–2 or Rule 25; (vi) more than two club-lengths from where it first struck the ground; or (vii) comes to rest nearer the hole than its original position unless otherwise permitted by the Rules.

Out of bounds

More than two club-lengths from point of striking ground

If the ball again rolls into such position, it shall be placed as near as possible to the spot where it first struck the ground when re-dropped. If a ball to be re-dropped or placed under this Rule is not immediately recoverable, another ball may be substituted. **Rule 20–2c.**

PLACING AND REPLACING

How and Where to Place

A ball to be placed under the Rules shall be placed by the player or his partner. A ball to be replaced shall be replaced by the player, his partner or the person who lifted or moved it. **Rule 20–3a.**

Spot Not Determinable

If it is impossible to determine the spot where the ball is to be placed:

(i) *through the green,* the ball shall be dropped as near as possible to the place where it lay but not nearer the hole or in a *hazard;*

(ii) in a hazard, the ball shall be dropped in the hazard as near as possible to the place where it lay but not nearer the hole;

(iii) on the *putting green,* the ball shall be placed as near as possible to the place where it lay but not nearer the hole or in a hazard. **Rule 20–3c.**

Ball Fails to Remain on Spot

If a ball when placed fails to remain on the spot on which it was placed, it shall be replaced without penalty. If it still fails to remain on that spot:

(i) except in a *hazard,* it shall be placed at the nearest spot not nearer the hole or in a hazard where it can be placed at rest;

(ii) in a hazard, it shall be placed in the hazard at the nearest spot not nearer the hole where it can be placed at rest. **Rule 20–3d.**

When Ball Dropped or Placed Is in Play

If the player's *ball in play* has been lifted, it is again in play when dropped or placed.

A substituted ball becomes the ball in play if it is dropped or placed under an applicable Rule, whether or not such Rule permits substitution. A ball substituted under an inapplicable Rule is a *wrong ball.* **Rule 20–4.**

LIE OF BALL TO BE PLACED OR REPLACED ALTERED

"Please lift your ball. It interferes with me."

Player A

A's ball

B's ball

Player B

B's lie is altered

Player B

If the original lie of a ball to be placed or replaced has been altered:

(i) except in a *hazard*, the ball shall be placed in the nearest lie most similar to the original lie which is not more than one club-length from the original lie, not nearer the hole and not in a hazard;

(ii) in a *water hazard*, the ball shall be placed in accordance with Clause (i) above, except that the ball must be placed in the water hazard;

(iii) in a *bunker*, the original lie shall be recreated as nearly as possible and the ball shall be placed in that lie. **Rule 20–3b.**

PLAYING NEXT STROKE FROM WHERE PREVIOUS STROKE PLAYED

"I've hit my shot out of bounds. I'll have to put another ball in play. Do I drop it or place it?"

"You are through the green, so you drop it."

When, under the Rules, a player elects or is required to play his next *stroke* from where a previous stroke was played, he shall proceed as follows: If the stroke is to be played from the *teeing ground,* the ball to be played shall be played from anywhere within the teeing ground and may be teed; if the stroke is to be played from *through the green* or a *hazard,* it shall be dropped; if the stroke is to be played on the *putting green,* it shall be placed. **Rule 20–5.**

LIFTING BALL WRONGLY DROPPED OR PLACED

A ball dropped or placed in a wrong place or otherwise not in accordance with the Rules but not played may be lifted, without penalty, and the player shall then proceed correctly. **Rule 20–6.**

"You dropped in the wrong place. But since you haven't played the ball you can lift it and drop correctly."

CLEANING BALL

"Now that I've lifted my ball may I clean it?"

"No, because you lifted it to identify it."

"May I remove the blade of grass from my ball?"

"No, since it adheres to your ball, it is not a loose impediment."

A ball on the putting green may be cleaned when lifted under Rule 16–1b. Elsewhere, a ball may be cleaned when lifted except when it has been lifted:

a. To determine if it is unfit for play (Rule 5–3);

b. For identification (Rule 12–2), in which case it may be cleaned only to the extent necessary for identification; or

c. Because it is interfering with or assisting play (Rule 22).

If a player cleans his ball during play of a hole except as provided in this Rule, *he shall incur a penalty of one stroke* and the ball, if lifted, shall be replaced.

If a player who is required to replace a ball fails to do so, *he shall incur the penalty* for breach of Rule 20–3a, but no additional penalty under Rule 21 shall be applied.

Exception: If a player incurs a penalty for failing to act in accordance with Rules 5–3, 12–2 or 22 no additional penalty under Rule 21 shall be applied. **Rule 21.**

BALL INTERFERING WITH OR ASSISTING PLAY

Ball Interfering

B's ball

Player B

A's ball

Player A

Ball Assisting

"Jim, wait until I lift my ball."

Jim

Any player may: (a) lift his ball if he considers that it might assist any other player, or (b) have any other ball lifted if he considers that it might interfere with his play or assist the play of any other player, but this may not be done while another ball is in motion. In stroke play, a player required to lift his ball may play first rather than lift. A ball lifted under this Rule shall be replaced.

If a ball is accidentally moved in complying with this Rule, no penalty is incurred and the ball shall be replaced. **Rule 22.**

LOOSE IMPEDIMENTS

May the twig be removed? Yes, since the ball does not lie in a hazard, but . . . There's a penalty if the ball moves unless the ball is lying on the putting green.

Relief

Except when both the *loose impediment* and the ball lie in or touch a *hazard,* any loose impediment may be removed without penalty. If the ball moves, see Rule 18–2c below.

When a player's ball is in motion, a loose impediment on his line of play shall not be removed. **Rule 23–1.** PENALTY for breach of Rule: *Match play—Loss of hole; Stroke play—Two strokes.*

(Searching for ball in hazard—Rule 12–1.)

(Touching line of putt—Rule 16–1a.)

Ball Moving After Loose Impediment Touched

Through the green, if the ball *moves* after any *loose impediment* lying within a club-length of it has been touched by the player, his partner or either of their caddies and before the player has *addressed* it, the player shall be deemed to have moved the ball and *shall incur a PENALTY stroke.* The player shall replace the ball unless the movement of the ball occurs after the player has begun his swing and he does not discontinue his swing.

On the *putting green,* if the ball moves in the process of removing any *loose impediment,* it shall be replaced without penalty. **Rule 18–2c.**

OBSTRUCTIONS
MOVABLE OBSTRUCTIONS

A player may obtain relief from a movable *obstruction* as follows:

a. If the ball does not lie in or on the obstruction, the obstruction may be removed; if the ball moves, no penalty is incurred and the ball shall be replaced.

b. If the ball lies in or on the obstruction, the ball may be lifted, without penalty, and the obstruction removed. The ball shall *through the green* or in *a hazard* be dropped, or on the *putting green* be placed, as near as possible to the spot directly under the place where the ball lay in or on the obstruction, but not nearer the hole. **Rule 24–1.**

IMMOVABLE OBSTRUCTIONS

Interference by an immovable obstruction occurs when a ball lies in or on the obstruction, or so close to the obstruction that the obstruction interferes with the player's *stance* or the area of his intended swing. A player may obtain relief from interference by an immovable *obstruction*, without penalty, as follows:

(i) *Through the green,* the point nearest to where the ball lies shall be determined (without crossing over, through or under the obstruction) which (1) is not nearer the hole, (2) avoids interference (as defined), and (3) is not in a *hazard* or on a *putting green*. The player shall lift the ball and drop it within one club-length of the point thus determined on ground which fulfills (1), (2) and (3) above.

Note: The prohibition against crossing over, through or under the *obstruction* does not apply to the artificial surfaces and sides of roads and paths or when the ball lies in or on the obstruction.

(ii) *In a bunker,* the player shall lift and drop the ball in accordance with Clause (i) above, except that the ball must be dropped in the *bunker.*

(iii) *On the putting green,* the player shall lift and place the ball in the nearest position to where it lay which affords relief from interference, but not nearer the hole nor in a hazard.

Exception: A player may not obtain relief under Rule 24–2b if (a) it is clearly unreasonable for him to play a stroke because of interference by anything other than an immovable obstruction or (b) interference by an immovable obstruction would occur only through use of an unnecessarily abnormal stance, swing or direction of play. .

Note: If a ball lies in or touches a *water hazard* (including a *lateral water hazard*), the player is not entitled to relief without penalty from interference by an immovable obstruction. The player shall play the ball as it lies or proceed under Rule 26–1. **Rule 24–2b.** PENALTY for breach of Rule: *Match play—Loss of hole; Stroke play—Two strokes.*

RELIEF FROM PAVED CART PATH

The ball is in such position that the paved cart path (an obstruction) interferes with the player's stance. Although Rule 24–2b in general prohibits crossing over the obstruction in determining the nearest point of relief, the prohibition does not apply to paved paths—(see Note). Thus, the player, if he desires relief, must drop the ball within one club-length of point X, the nearest point of relief not nearer the hole.

NO RELIEF FOR LINE OF PLAY ALONE

The ball lies so far behind the shelter house that it does not interfere with the player's swing. The player is not entitled to drop his ball so as to avoid the shelter house on line to the green. Rule 24-2a provides in these circumstances that intervention on the line of play is not, of itself, interference under this Rule.

ABNORMAL GROUND CONDITIONS AND WRONG PUTTING GREEN

RELIEF FROM CASUAL WATER OR GROUND UNDER REPAIR

Interference by *casual water, ground under repair,* or a hole, cast or runway made by a burrowing animal, a reptile or a bird occurs when a ball lies in or touches any of these conditions or when the condition interferes with the player's stance or the area of his intended swing. If the player's ball lies on the *putting green,* interference also occurs if such condition or the putting green intervenes on his line of putt. If interference exists, the player may either play the ball as it lies or take relief as follows:

On the Putting Green

Ball A lies on the putting green with casual water intervening between it and the hole. *Ball A* may be lifted without penalty and placed at nearby point X, which is the nearest position to where it lay which affords maximum relief from the casual water, but not nearer the hole. (If *Ball A* were lying *in* casual water on the putting green, similar relief would be available.) **Rule 25–1b (iii).**

Ball B lies off the putting green. The player is not entitled to relief from casual water lying on the putting green which intervenes between *Ball B* and the hole.

Through the Green

Ball C lies in ground under repair, in an area normally "fairway." *Ball C* may be lifted and dropped without penalty outside the ground under repair within one club-length of X, the nearest point which (a) is not nearer the hole, (b) avoids interference by the condition, and (c) is not in a hazard or on a putting green. **Rule 25–1b(i).** (The permissible drop area is in the "rough," but the Rules do not distinguish between "fairway" and "rough"—both are "through the green," according to definition.)

Ball D lies so near to casual water that a right-handed player would be obliged to stand in casual water. He may lift and drop the ball without penalty outside the casual water, within one club-length of the nearest point of relief not nearer the hole. The point is indicated by the X.

PENALTY for breach of Rule: *Match play—Loss of hole; Stroke play—Two strokes.*

CASUAL WATER IN BUNKER

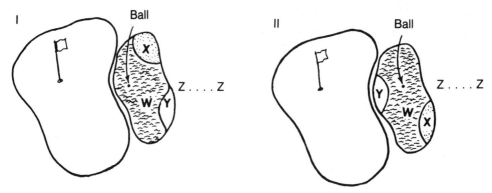

Area W—water three inches deep; *Area X*—water one-eighth inch deep; *Area Y*—no casual water.

I. The player would like to drop the ball in area X. However, he may drop only:
    1. At nearest point in area Y, without penalty, or
    2. Along line Z . . . Z behind the bunker, under penalty of one stroke.

II. The player may drop the ball at either:
    1. The nearest point in area X, without penalty, or
    2. Along line Z . . . Z behind the bunker, under penalty of one stroke. He may not drop in area Y as it is nearer the hole than the ball's original position.

In a bunker, if there is interference by casual water, ground under repair, or a hole, cast or runway made by a burrowing animal, a reptile or a bird, the player may lift and drop the ball either:

Without penalty, in the bunker as near as possible to the spot where his ball lay, but not nearer the hole, on ground which affords maximum relief from the condition;

or

Under penalty of one stroke, outside the bunker, keeping the point where the ball lay directly between the hole and the spot on which the ball is dropped.

PENALTY for breach of Rule: *Match play—Loss of hole; Stroke play—Two strokes.* **Rule 25–1b(ii).**

BALL LOST IN CASUAL WATER OR GROUND UNDER REPAIR

"I'm sure my ball went in here, but I can't find it."

In order that a ball may be treated as lost under a condition covered by Rule 25, there must be reasonable evidence to that effect. If a ball is lost under such condition through the green, the player may take relief as follows: The point nearest to where the ball last crossed the margin of the area shall be determined which (a) is not nearer the hole than where the ball last crossed the margin, (b) avoids interference by the condition, and (c) is not in a hazard or on a putting green. He shall drop a ball without penalty within one club-length of the point thus determined on ground which fulfills (a), (b) and (c) above. **Rule 25–1c.** PENALTY for breach of Rule: *Match play—Loss of hole; Stroke play—Two strokes.*

EMBEDDED BALL

Ball in fairway

Ball in rough

A ball embedded in its own pitch-mark in the ground in any closely mown area *through the green* may be lifted, cleaned and dropped, without penalty, as near as possible to the spot where it lay but not nearer the hole. "Closely mown area" means any area of the *course,* including paths through the rough, cut to fairway height or less. **Rule 25–2.**

BALL ON A WRONG PUTTING GREEN

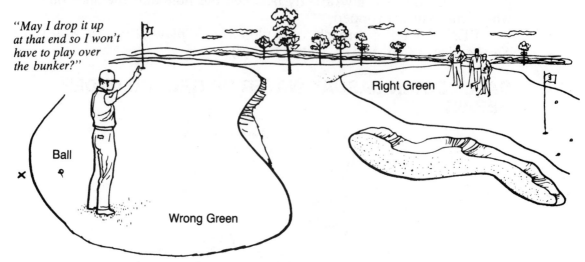

"May I drop it up at that end so I won't have to play over the bunker?"

Right Green

Ball

x

Wrong Green

If a ball lies on a *putting green* other than that of the hole being played, the point on the *course* nearest to where the ball lies shall be determined which (a) is not nearer the hole and (b) is not in a *hazard* or on a putting green. The player shall lift the ball and drop it without penalty within one club-length of the point thus determined on ground which fulfills (a) and (b) above. In the illustration, the player must drop off the green within one club-length of point X.

WATER HAZARDS (INCLUDING LATERAL WATER HAZARDS)

BALL IN WATER HAZARD—PROCEDURE

Player T's ball lies in the water hazard in front of green. He may drop a ball, under penalty of one stroke, either:

a. Behind the water hazard, keeping the point (C) at which the original ball last crossed the margin of the water hazard directly between the hole and the spot on which the ball is dropped, with no limit to how far behind the water hazard the ball may be dropped (the line of dropping is X—X—X—X);

or

b. As near as possible to the spot from which the original ball was played; if the stroke was played from the teeing ground, the ball may be teed anywhere within the teeing ground. **Rule 26–1.**

Player Q's ball has entered the lateral water hazard at left. He may, under penalty of one stroke, either:

a. Drop a ball behind the lateral water hazard, keeping the point (D) at which the original ball last crossed the margin of the lateral water hazard directly between the hole and the spot on which the ball is dropped, with no limit to how far behind the lateral water hazard the ball may be dropped (the line of dropping is Z—Z—Z—Z);

□ MARGIN OF WATER HAZARD

• MARGIN OF LATERAL WATER HAZARD

Thus, brook between A-A and B-B is lateral water hazard; other parts of brook are regular water hazard. C and D—spots where balls last crossed hazard margin.

 or

 b. Drop a ball as near as possible to the spot from which the original ball was played; if the stroke was played from the teeing ground, the ball may be teed anywhere within the teeing ground;

 or

 c. Drop a ball outside the hazard within two club-lengths of the point (D) where the ball last crossed the hazard margin or a point on the opposite margin of the hazard equidistant from the hole. The ball must be dropped and come to rest not nearer the hole than point D. Thus, Player Q may drop a ball on either area marked E. **Rule 26–1.**

 PENALTY for breach of Rule: *Match play—Loss of hole; Stroke play—Two strokes.*

DOUBT WHETHER BALL IN WATER HAZARD

"If my ball is lost in the water hazard, I can save distance."

It is a question of fact whether a ball lost after having been struck toward a water hazard is lost inside or outside the hazard. In order to treat the ball as lost in the hazard, there must be reasonable evidence that the ball lodged therein. In the absence of such evidence, the ball must be treated as a lost ball and Rule 27 applies.

BALL PLAYED WITHIN WATER HAZARD

a. *Ball Comes to Rest in Hazard*

If a ball played from within a water hazard comes to rest in the hazard after the stroke, the player may:

(i) proceed under Rule 26–1; or

(ii) *under penalty of one stroke,* play his next stroke as nearly as possible at the spot from which the last stroke from outside the hazard was played (see Rule 20–5).

b. *Ball Lost or Unplayable Outside Hazard or Out of Bounds*

If a ball played from within a water hazard is lost or declared unplayable outside the hazard or is out of bounds, the player, after taking *a penalty of one stroke* under Rule 27–1 or 28a, may:

(i) play a ball as nearly as possible at the spot in the hazard from which the original ball was last played (see Rule 20–5); or

(ii) *under an additional penalty of one stroke,* proceed under Rule 26–1b or, if applicable, Rule 26–1c, using as the reference point the point where the original ball last crossed the margin of the hazard before it came to rest in the hazard; or

(iii) *under an additional penalty of one stroke,* play his next stroke as nearly as possible at the spot from which the last stroke from outside the hazard was played (see Rule 20–5).

Note: If a ball played from within a water hazard is declared unplayable outside the hazard, nothing in Rule 26–2b precludes the player from proceeding under Rule 28b or c. **Rule 26–2.**

PENALTY for breach of Rule: *Match play—Loss of hole; Stroke play—Two strokes.*

BALL LOST; OUT OF BOUNDS; OR UNPLAYABLE

BALL LOST OR OUT OF BOUNDS

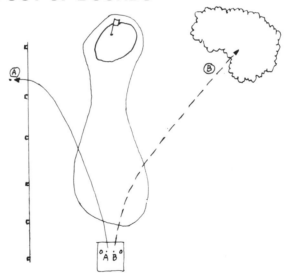

Out of Bounds

Player A's ball is out of bounds. He must replay from the tee, count both strokes made and add a penalty stroke to his score for the hole. **Rule 27–1.**

Lost

Player B is unable to find his ball in the thick underbrush. His only procedure for a lost ball is to play again from the tee, count both strokes played and add a penalty stroke to his score for the hole. **Rule 27–1.**

PENALTY for breach of Rule: *Match play—Loss of hole; Stroke play—Two strokes.*

PROVISIONAL BALL

"*That may be lost or out of bounds. I'll play a provisional.*"

"*That could be unplayable in the pond. Is a provisional allowed?*"

"*Sorry—not for that reason.*"

If a ball may be *lost* outside a *water hazard* or may be *out of bounds,* to save time the player may play another ball provisionally as nearly as possible at the spot from which the original ball was played—see Rule 20–5. The player shall inform his opponent in match play or his marker or a fellow-competitor in stroke play that he intends to play a *provisional ball,* and he shall play it before he or his partner goes forward to search for the original ball. If he fails to do so, and plays another ball, such ball is not a provisional ball and becomes the *ball in play* under penalty of stroke and distance (Rule 27–1); the original ball is deemed to be lost. **Rule 27–2.**

WHEN PROVISIONAL BALL BECOMES BALL IN PLAY

"That puts the provisional ball in play."

Original ball

Provisional ball

"That's unplayable. I'll have to give up the provisional ball, too."

Original ball

Provisional ball

The player may play a provisional ball until he reaches the place where the original ball is likely to be. If he plays a stroke with the provisional ball from the place where the original ball is likely to be or from a point nearer the hole than that place, the original ball is deemed to be *lost,* and the provisional ball becomes the ball in play *under penalty of stroke and distance.*

If the original ball is lost outside a water hazard or is out of bounds, the provisional ball becomes the ball in play, *under penalty of stroke and distance* (Rule 27–1). **Rule 27–2b.**

If the original ball is neither lost outside a water hazard nor out of bounds, the player shall abandon the provisional ball and continue play with the original ball. If he fails to do so, any further strokes played with the provisional ball shall constitute playing a *wrong ball* and the provisions of Rule 15 shall apply. **Rule 27–2c.**

Note: If the original ball lies in a water hazard, the player shall play the ball as it lies or proceed under Rule 26. If it is lost in a water hazard or unplayable, the player shall proceed under Rule 26 or 28, whichever is applicable.

BALL UNPLAYABLE

Player C finds his ball at the base of a thick, bushy tree. He declares it unplayable under Rule 28 (the player may declare his ball unplayable at any place on the course except when the ball lies in or touches a *water hazard*). He has three options for relief:

1. He may play again from the tee under penalty of one stroke (see Rule 20–5).

2. He may drop a ball, under penalty of one stroke, either:

(a) Within two club-lengths of the point where the ball lay, but not nearer the hole (shaded area Z), or

(b) Behind the unplayable lie on line XXX so as to keep the point where the ball lies unplayable directly between the hole and the spot on which the ball is dropped, with no limit to how far behind that point the ball may be dropped. (If the ball lies in a bunker and Player C elects to proceed under option 2(a) or 2(b), he would have to drop in the bunker). **Rule 28.**

PENALTY for breach of Rule: *Match play—Loss of hole; Stroke play—Two strokes.*

OTHER FORMS OF PLAY

THREESOMES AND FOURSOMES

The woman has hit the ball into the water hazard and she and her partner wish to drop a ball behind the hazard under penalty of one stroke (Rule 26–1). Who should play the next stroke, the man or his partner?

The man must play the next stroke because a penalty stroke does not affect the order of play.

General

In a threesome or a foursome, during any *stipulated round* the partners shall play alternately from the teeing grounds and alternately during the play of each hole. *Penalty strokes* do not affect the order of play. **Rule 29–1.**

Match Play

If a player plays when his partner should have played, *his side shall lose the hole.* **Rule 29–2.**

Stroke Play

If the partners play a stroke or strokes in incorrect order, such stroke or strokes shall be cancelled and *the side shall incur a penalty of two strokes.* The side shall correct the error by playing a ball in correct order at the spot from which it first played in incorrect order (see Rule 20–5). If the side plays a stroke from the next *teeing ground* without first correcting the error or, in the case of the last hole of the round, leaves the *putting green* without declaring its intention to correct the error, *the side shall be disqualified.* **Rule 29–3.**

FOUR-BALL MATCH AND STROKE PLAY

"My partner's not here, so I'll represent our side."

Representation of Side

A side may be represented by one partner for all or any part of a match or stipulated round; all partners need not be present. An absent partner may join a match between holes, but not during play of a hole. **Rules 30–3a** and **31–2.**

ORDER OF PLAY

"You putt first, partner, so I can get some idea about the line."

Match Play and Stroke Play

Balls belonging to the same side may be played in the order the side considers best. **Rules 30–3c** and **31–5.**

BREACH AFFECTING OTHER PLAYER

"You're not allowed to remove loose impediments in a hazard. We are both penalized."

Player A   Player B

If a player's breach of a Rule assists his partner's play, or in match play adversely affects an opponent's play, *the partner incurs the relative penalty in addition to any penalty incurred by the player.* **Rules 30–3f** and **31–8.**

THE COMMITTEE

COMBINING MATCH AND STROKE PLAY PROHIBITED

"Can't we kill two birds with one stone today—play our match in the club championship and also compete in the weekly medal play?"

"No—it wouldn't be right."

Certain special rules governing stroke play are so substantially different from those governing match play that combining the two forms of play is not practicable and is not permitted. The results of matches played and the scores returned in these circumstances shall not be accepted. **Rule 33–1.**

DEFINING BOUNDS AND MARGINS

"Am I in a water hazard or not?"

The Committee shall define accurately:
a. The *course* and *out of bounds.*
b. The margins of *water hazards* and *lateral water hazards.*
c. *Ground under repair.*
d. *Obstructions* and integral parts of the course. **Rule 33–2a.**

COURSE UNPLAYABLE

If the Committee or its authorized representative considers that for any reason the course is not in a playable condition or that there are circumstances which render the proper playing of the game impossible, it may, in match or stroke play, order a temporary suspension of play or, in stroke play, declare play null and void and cancel all scores for the round in question.

When play has been temporarily suspended, it shall be resumed from where it was discontinued, even though resumption occurs on a subsequent day. When a round is canceled, all penalties incurred in that round are canceled. **Rule 33–2d.**

(Procedure in discontinuing play—see Rule 6–8.)

LOCAL RULE WAIVING PENALTY

"There's a Local Rule here— no penalty for dropping out of a water hazard. That's wrong."

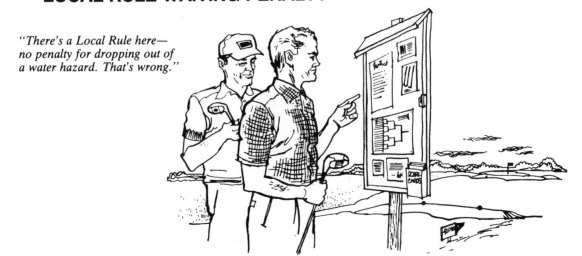

A penalty imposed by a Rule of Golf shall not be waived by a Local Rule. **Rule 33–8b.**

HOW TO USE THE RULES BOOK

To familiarize yourself with the Rules book, first study the Table of Contents at the front to get an idea of how the Rules are organized. Then look at the captions under each Rule to see the matters covered and the order in which they are treated. Having done this, it is hoped that most of the time you will be able to find the relevant Rule simply by reference to the Table of Contents. If not, there is an Index on pages 120-134 which should lead you to the relevant Rule.

The following suggestions are offered for learning how to apply the Rules of Golf to specific cases:

l. Identify the form of play. Match play or stroke play? The penalties differ significantly. Single, foursome or four-ball? (A foursome and a four-ball are not the same thing.) Singles match play and individual stroke play are covered in Rules 1-28. These Rules, as supplemented and modified by Rules 29-32, govern threesomes and foursomes, multi-ball match play and stroke play and bogey, par and Stableford competitions.

2. Who is involved? The player, his partner or his caddie? In match play, the player's opponent or his caddie? In stroke play, a fellow-competitor or his caddie? Or an outside agency?

3. Where did the incident occur? On the teeing ground of the hole being played? In a hazard (*i.e.*, a bunker, a water hazard or a lateral water hazard)? On the putting green of the hole being played? Or elsewhere on the course (*i.e.*, "through the green")? Where the incident occurs can have a significant effect on what the player may do or the relief to which he is entitled.

4. Pay attention to the Definitions set forth in full in alphabetical order at the front of the book. Definitions are repeated at the beginning of each Rule in which they are used and are likely to be important to the correct application of the Rule. Defined terms which may be significant are underscored the first time they appear in a Rule.

5. Carry a Rules book in your golf bag and use it whenever a question arises. Knowing the Rules may enable you not only to avoid penalties but also to save strokes.

THE RULES OF GOLF

Section I
ETIQUETTE

Courtesy on the Course

Safety

Prior to playing a stroke or making a practice swing, the player should ensure that no one is standing close by or in a position to be hit by the club, the ball or any stones, pebbles, twigs or the like which may be moved by the stroke or swing.

Consideration for Other Players

The player who has the honor should be allowed to play before his opponent or fellow-competitor tees his ball.

No one should move, talk or stand close to or directly behind the ball or the hole when a player is addressing the ball or making a stroke.

In the interest of all, players should play without delay.

No player should play until the players in front are out of range.

Players searching for a ball should signal the players behind them to pass as soon as it becomes apparent that the ball will not easily be found. They should not search for five minutes before doing so. They should not continue play until the players following them have passed and are out of range.

When the play of a hole has been completed, players should immediately leave the putting green.

Priority on the Course

In the absence of special rules, two-ball matches should have precedence over and be entitled to pass any three- or four-ball match.

A single player has no standing and should give way to a match of any kind.

Any match playing a whole round is entitled to pass a match playing a shorter round.

If a match fails to keep its place on the course and loses more than one clear hole on the players in front, it should invite the match following to pass.

Care of the Course

Holes in Bunkers

Before leaving a bunker, a player should carefully fill up and smooth over all holes and footprints made by him.

Replace Divots; Repair Ball-Marks and Damage by Spikes

Through the green, a player should ensure that any turf cut or displaced by him is replaced at once and pressed down and that any damage to the putting green made by a ball is carefully repaired. Damage to the putting green caused by golf shoe spikes should be repaired *on completion of the hole.*

Damage to Greens — Flagsticks, Bags, etc.

Players should ensure that, when putting down bags or the flagstick, no damage is done to the putting green and that neither they nor their caddies damage the hole by standing close to it, in handling the flagstick or in removing the ball from the hole. The flagstick should be properly replaced in the hole before the players leave the putting green. Players should not damage the putting green by leaning on their putters, particularly when removing the ball from the hole.

Golf Carts

Local notices regulating the movement of golf carts should be strictly observed.

Damage Through Practice Swings

In taking practice swings, players should avoid causing damage to the course, particularly the tees, by removing divots.

Section II
DEFINITIONS

Addressing the Ball

A player has "addressed the ball" when he has taken his stance and has also grounded his club, except that in a hazard a player has addressed the ball when he has taken his stance.

Advice

"Advice" is any counsel or suggestion which could influence a player in determining his play, the choice of a club or the method of making a stroke.

Information on the Rules or on matters of public information, such as the position of hazards or the flagstick on the putting green, is not advice.

Ball Deemed to Move

See "Move or Moved."

Ball Holed

See "Holed."

Ball Lost

See "Lost Ball."

Ball in Play

A ball is "in play" as soon as the player has made a stroke on the teeing ground. It remains in play until holed out, except when it is lost, out of bounds or lifted, or another ball has been substituted under an applicable Rule, whether or not such Rule permits substitution; a ball so substituted becomes the ball in play.

Bunker

A "bunker" is a hazard consisting of a prepared area of ground, often a hollow, from which turf or soil has been removed and replaced with sand or the like. Grass-covered ground bordering or within a bunker is not part of the bunker. The margin of a bunker extends vertically downwards, but not upwards.

Caddie
A "caddie" is one who carries or handles a player's clubs during play and otherwise assists him in accordance with the Rules.

When one caddie is employed by more than one player, he is always deemed to be the caddie of the player whose ball is involved, and equipment carried by him is deemed to be that player's equipment, except when the caddie acts upon specific directions of another player, in which case he is considered to be that other player's caddie.

Casual Water
"Casual water" is any temporary accumulation of water on the course which is visible before or after the player takes his stance and is not in a water hazard. Snow and ice are either casual water or loose impediments, at the option of the player, except that manufactured ice is an obstruction. Dew is not casual water.

Committee
The "Committee" is the committee in charge of the competition or, if the matter does not arise in a competition, the committee in charge of the course.

Competitor
A "competitor" is a player in a stroke competition. A "fellow-competitor" is any person with whom the competitor plays. Neither is partner of the other.

In stroke play foursome and four-ball competitions, where the context so admits, the word "competitor" or "fellow-competitor" includes his partner.

Course
The "course" is the whole area within which play is permitted. See Rule 33-2.

Equipment
"Equipment" is anything used, worn or carried by or for the player except any ball he has played at the hole being played and any small object, such as a coin or a tee, when used to mark the position of a ball or the extent of an area in which a ball is to be dropped. Equipment includes a golf cart, whether or not motorized. If such a cart is shared by more than one player, its status under the Rules is the same as that of a caddie employed by more than one player. See "Caddie."

Fellow-Competitor
See "Competitor."

Flagstick
The "flagstick" is a movable straight indicator, with or without bunting or other material attached, centered in the hole to show its position. It shall be circular in cross-section.

Forecaddie
A "forecaddie" is one who is employed by the Committee to indicate to players the position of balls during play. He is an outside agency.

Ground Under Repair
"Ground under repair" is any portion of the course so marked by order of the Committee or so declared by its authorized representative. It includes material piled for removal and a hole made by a greenkeeper, even if not so marked. Stakes and lines defining ground under repair are in such ground. The margin of ground under repair extends vertically downwards, but not upwards.

Note 1: Grass cuttings and other material left on the course which have been abandoned and are not intended to be removed are not ground under repair unless so marked.

Note 2: The Committee may make a Local Rule prohibiting play from ground under repair.

Hazards
A "hazard" is any bunker or water hazard.

Hole
The "hole" shall be 4¼ inches (108mm) in diameter and at least 4 inches (100mm) deep. If a lining is used, it shall be sunk at least 1 inch (25mm) below the putting green surface unless the nature of the soil makes it impracticable to do so; its outer diameter shall not exceed 4¼ inches (108mm).

Holed
A ball is "holed" when it is at rest within the circumference of the hole and all of it is below the level of the lip of the hole.

Honor
The side entitled to play first from the teeing ground is said to have the "honor."

Lateral Water Hazard
A "lateral water hazard" is a water hazard or that part of a water hazard so situated that it is not possible or is deemed by the Committee to be impracticable to drop a ball behind the water hazard in accordance with Rule 26-1b.

That part of a water hazard to be played as a lateral water hazard should be distinctively marked.

Note: Lateral water hazards should be defined by red stakes or lines.

Loose Impediments
"Loose impediments" are natural objects such as stones, leaves, twigs, branches and the like, dung, worms and insects and casts or heaps made by them, provided they are not fixed or growing, are not solidly embedded and do not adhere to the ball.

Sand and loose soil are loose impediments on the putting green, but not elsewhere.

Snow and ice are either casual water or loose impediments, at the option of the player, except that manufactured ice is an obstruction.

Dew is not a loose impediment.

Lost Ball
A ball is "lost" if:

a. It is not found or identified as his by the player within five minutes after the player's side or his or their caddies have begun to search for it; or

b. The player has put another ball into play under the Rules, even though he may not have searched for the original ball; or

c. The player has played any stroke with a provisional ball from the place where the original ball is likely to be or from a point nearer the hole than that place, whereupon the provisional ball becomes the ball in play.

Time spent in playing a wrong ball is not counted in the five-minute period allowed for search.

Marker
A "marker" is one who is appointed by the Committee to record a competitor's score in stroke play. He may be a fellow-competitor. He is not a referee.

Matches
See "Sides and Matches."

Move or Moved
A ball is deemed to have "moved" if it leaves its position and comes to rest in any other place.

Observer
An "observer" is one who is appointed by the Committee to assist a referee to decide questions of fact and to report to him any breach of a Rule. An observer should not attend the flagstick, stand at or mark the position of the hole, or lift the ball or mark its position.

Obstructions
An "obstruction" is anything artificial, including the artificial surfaces and sides of roads and paths and manufactured ice, except:

a. Objects defining out of bounds, such as walls, fences, stakes and railings;

b. Any part of an immovable artificial object which is out of bounds; and

c. Any construction declared by the Committee to be an integral part of the course.

Out of Bounds

"Out of bounds" is ground on which play is prohibited.

When out of bounds is defined by reference to stakes or a fence or as being beyond stakes or a fence, the out of bounds line is determined by the nearest inside points of the stakes or fence posts at ground level excluding angled supports.

When out of bounds is defined by a line on the ground, the line itself is out of bounds.

The out of bounds line extends vertically upwards and downwards.

A ball is out of bounds when all of it lies out of bounds.

A player may stand out of bounds to play a ball lying within bounds.

Outside Agency

An "outside agency" is any agency not part of the match or, in stroke play, not part of a competitor's side, and includes a referee, a marker, an observer or a fore-caddie. Neither wind nor water is an outside agency.

Partner

A "partner" is a player associated with another player on the same side.

In a threesome, foursome, best-ball or four-ball match, where the context so admits, the word "player" includes his partner or partners.

Penalty Stroke

A "penalty stroke" is one added to the score of a player or side under certain Rules. In a threesome or foursome, penalty strokes do not affect the order of play.

Provisional Ball

A "provisional ball" is a ball played under Rule 27-2 for a ball which may be lost outside a water hazard or may be out of bounds.

Putting Green

The "putting green" is all ground of the hole being played which is specially prepared for putting or otherwise defined as such by the Committee. A ball is on the putting green when any part of it touches the putting green.

Referee

A "referee" is one who is appointed by the Committee to accompany players to decide questions of fact and apply the Rules of Golf. He shall act on any breach of a Rule which he observes or is reported to him.

A referee should not attend the flagstick, stand at or mark the position of the hole, or lift the ball or mark its position.

Rub of the Green

A "rub of the green" occurs when a ball in motion is accidentally deflected or stopped by any outside agency (see Rule 19-1).

Rule

The term "Rule" includes Local Rules made by the Committee under Rule 33-8a.

Sides and Matches

Side: A player, or two or more players who are partners.
Single: A match in which one plays against another.

Threesome: A match in which one plays against two, and each side plays one ball.

Foursome: A match in which two play against two, and each side plays one ball.

Three-Ball: A match play competition in which three play against one another, each playing his own ball. Each player is playing two distinct matches.

Best-Ball: A match in which one plays against the better ball of two or the best ball of three players.

Four-Ball: A match in which two play their better ball against the better ball of two other players.

Stance

Taking the "stance" consists in a player placing his feet in position for and preparatory to making a stroke.

Stipulated Round

The "stipulated round" consists of playing the holes of the course in their correct sequence unless otherwise authorized by the Committee. The number of holes in a stipulated round is 18 unless a smaller number is authorized by the Committee. As to extension of stipulated round in match play, see Rule 2-3.

Stroke

A "stroke" is the forward movement of the club made with the intention of fairly striking at and moving the ball, but if a player checks his downswing voluntarily before the clubhead reaches the ball he is deemed not to have made a stroke.

Teeing Ground

The "teeing ground" is the starting place for the hole to be played. It is a rectangular area two club-lengths in depth, the front and the sides of which are defined by the outside limits of two tee-markers. A ball is outside the teeing ground when all of it lies outside the teeing ground.

Through the Green

"Through the green" is the whole area of the course except:

a. The teeing ground and putting green of the hole being played; and

b. All hazards on the course.

Water Hazard

A "water hazard" is any sea, lake, pond, river, ditch, surface drainage ditch or other open water course (whether or not containing water) and anything of a similar nature.

All ground or water within the margin of a water hazard is part of the water hazard. The margin of a water hazard extends vertically upwards and downwards. Stakes and lines defining the margins of water hazards are in the hazards.

Note: Water hazards (other than lateral water hazards) should be defined by yellow stakes or lines.

Wrong Ball

A "wrong ball" is any ball other than:

a. The ball in play,

b. A provisional ball or

c. In stroke play, a second ball played under Rule 3-3 or Rule 20-7b.

Note: Ball in play includes a ball substituted for the ball in play when the player is proceeding under an applicable Rule which does not permit substitution.

Section III
THE RULES OF PLAY

THE GAME
Rule 1. The Game

1-1. General

The Game of Golf consists in playing a ball from the teeing ground into the hole by a stroke or successive strokes in accordance with the Rules.

1-2. Exerting Influence on Ball

No player or caddie shall take any action to influence the position or the movement of a ball except in accordance with the Rules.

PENALTY FOR BREACH OF RULE 1-2:
Match play — Loss of hole; Stroke play — Two strokes.

Note: In the case of a serious breach of Rule 1-2, the Committee may impose a penalty of disqualification.

1-3. Agreement to Waive Rules

Players shall not agree to exclude the operation of any Rule or to waive any penalty incurred.

PENALTY FOR BREACH OF RULE 1-3:
Match play — Disqualification of both sides; Stroke play — Disqualification of competitors concerned.

(Agreeing to play out of turn in stroke play — see Rule 10-2c.)

1-4. Points Not Covered by Rules
If any point in dispute is not covered by the Rules, the decision shall be made in accordance with equity.

Rule 2. Match Play

2-1. Winner of Hole; Reckoning of Holes
In match play the game is played by holes.

Except as otherwise provided in the Rules, a hole is won by the side which holes its ball in the fewer strokes. In a handicap match the lower net score wins the hole.

The reckoning of holes is kept by the terms: so many "holes up" or "all square," and so many "to play."

A side is "dormie" when it is as many holes up as there are holes remaining to be played.

2-2. Halved Hole
A hole is halved if each side holes out in the same number of strokes.

When a player has holed out and his opponent has been left with a stroke for the half, if the player thereafter incurs a penalty, the hole is halved.

2-3. Winner of Match
A match (which consists of a stipulated round, unless otherwise decreed by the Committee) is won by the side which is leading by a number of holes greater than the number of holes remaining to be played.

The Committee may, for the purpose of settling a tie, extend the stipulated round to as many holes as are required for a match to be won.

2-4. Concession of Next Stroke, Hole or Match
When the opponent's ball is at rest or is deemed to be at rest under Rule 16-2, the player may concede the opponent to have holed out with his next stroke and the ball may be removed by either side with a club or otherwise.

A player may concede a hole or a match at any time prior to the conclusion of the hole or the match.

Concession of a stroke, hole or match may not be declined or withdrawn.

2-5. Claims
In match play, if a doubt or dispute arises between the players and no duly authorized representative of the Committee is available within a reasonable time, the players shall continue the match without delay. Any claim, if it is to be considered by the Committee, must be made before any player in the match plays from the next teeing ground or, in the case of the last hole of the match, before all players in the match leave the putting green.

No later claim shall be considered unless it is based on facts previously unknown to the player making the claim and the player making the claim had been given wrong information (Rules 6-2a and 9) by an opponent. In any case, no later claim shall be considered after the result of the match has been officially announced, unless the Committee is satisfied that the opponent knew he was giving wrong information.

2-6. General Penalty
The penalty for a breach of a Rule in match play is loss of hole except when otherwise provided.

Rule 3. Stroke Play

3-1. Winner
The competitor who plays the stipulated round or rounds in the fewest strokes is the winner.

3-2. Failure to Hole Out
If a competitor fails to hole out at any hole and does not correct his mistake before he plays a stroke from the next teeing ground or, in the case of the last hole of the round, before he leaves the putting green, *he shall be disqualified.*

3-3. Doubt as to Procedure

a. PROCEDURE
In stroke play only, when during play of a hole a competitor is doubtful of his rights or procedure, he may, without penalty, play a second ball. After the situation which caused the doubt has arisen, the competitor should, before taking further action, announce to his marker or a fellow-competitor his decision to invoke this Rule and the ball with which he will score if the Rules permit.

The competitor shall report the facts to the Committee before returning his score card unless he scores the same with both balls; if he fails to do so, *he shall be disqualified.*

b. DETERMINATION OF SCORE FOR HOLE
If the Rules allow the procedure selected in advance by the competitor, the score with the ball selected shall be his score for the hole.

If the competitor fails to announce in advance his decision to invoke this Rule or his selection, the score with the original ball or, if the original ball is not one of the balls being played, the first ball put into play shall count if the Rules allow the procedure adopted for such ball.

Note: A second ball played under Rule 3-3 is not a provisional ball under Rule 27-2.

3-4. Refusal to Comply with a Rule
If a competitor refuses to comply with a Rule affecting the rights of another competitor, *he shall be disqualified.*

3-5. General Penalty
The penalty for a breach of a Rule in stroke play is two strokes except when otherwise provided.

CLUBS AND THE BALL

The United States Golf Association and the Royal and Ancient Golf Club of St. Andrews reserve the right to change the Rules and make and change the interpretations relating to clubs, balls and other implements at any time.

Rule 4. Clubs

If there may be any reasonable basis for doubt as to whether a club which is to be manufactured conforms with Rule 4 and Appendix II, the manufacturer should submit a sample to the United States Golf Association for a ruling, such sample to become its property for reference purposes. If a manufacturer fails to do so, he assumes the risk of a ruling that the club does not conform with the Rules of Golf.

A player in doubt as to the conformity of a club should consult the United States Golf Association.

4-1. Form and Make of Clubs
A club is an implement designed to be used for striking the ball.

A putter is a club designed primarily for use on the putting green.

The player's clubs shall conform with the provisions of this Rule and with the specifications and interpretations set forth in Appendix II.

a. GENERAL
The club shall be composed of a shaft and a head. All parts of the club shall be fixed so that the club is one unit. The club shall not be designed to be adjustable except for weight. The club shall not be substantially different from the traditional and customary form and make.

b. SHAFT
The shaft shall be generally straight, with the same bending and twisting properties in any direction, and shall be attached to the clubhead at the heel either directly or through a single plain neck or socket. A putter shaft may be attached to any point in the head.

c. GRIP
The grip consists of that part of the shaft designed to be held by the player and any material added to it for the purpose of obtaining a firm hold. The grip shall be substantially straight and plain in form and shall not be molded for any part of the hands.

d. Clubhead

The distance from the heel to the toe of the clubhead shall be greater than the distance from the face to the back. The clubhead shall be generally plain in shape.

The clubhead shall have only one face designed for striking the ball, except that a putter may have two such faces if their characteristics are the same, they are opposite each other and the loft of each is the same and does not exceed 10 degrees.

e. Club Face

The face shall not have any degree of concavity and, in relation to the ball, shall be hard and rigid. It shall be generally smooth except for such markings as are permitted by Appendix II. If the basic structural material of the head and face of a club, other than a putter, is metal, no inset or attachment is permitted.

f. Wear

A club which conforms with Rule 4-1 when new is deemed to conform after wear through normal use. Any part of a club which has been purposely altered is regarded as new and must conform, in the altered state, with the Rules.

g. Damage

If a player's club ceases to conform with Rule 4-1 because of damage sustained in the normal course of play, the player may:

(i) use the club in its damaged state, but only for the remainder of the stipulated round during which such damage was sustained; or

(ii) without unduly delaying play, repair it.

A club which ceases to conform because of damage sustained other than in the normal course of play shall not subsequently be used during the round.

(Damage changing playing characteristics of club — see Rule 4-2.)

4-2. Playing Characteristics Changed

During a stipulated round, the playing characteristics of a club shall not be purposely changed.

If the playing characteristics of a player's club are changed during a round because of damage sustained in the normal course of play, the player may:

(i) use the club in its altered state; or

(ii) without unduly delaying play, repair it.

If the playing characteristics of a player's club are changed because of damage sustained other than in the normal course of play, the club shall not subsequently be used during the round.

Damage to a club which occurred prior to a round may be repaired during the round, provided the playing characteristics are not changed and play is not unduly delayed.

4-3. Foreign Material

No foreign material shall be applied to the club face for the purpose of influencing the movement of the ball.

PENALTY FOR BREACH OF RULE 4-1, -2 or -3:
Disqualification.

4-4. Maximum of Fourteen Clubs

a. Selection and Replacement of Clubs

The player shall start a stipulated round with not more than fourteen clubs. He is limited to the clubs thus selected for that round except that, without unduly delaying play, he may:

(i) if he started with fewer than fourteen, add as many as will bring his total to that number; and

(ii) replace, with any club, a club which becomes unfit for play in the normal course of play.

b. Borrowing or Sharing Clubs

The addition or replacement of a club or clubs may be made by borrowing from anyone; only the borrower may use such club or clubs for the remainder of the round.

The sharing of a club or clubs is prohibited except that partners may share clubs, provided that the total number of clubs carried by the partners so sharing does not exceed fourteen.

PENALTY FOR BREACH OF RULE 4-4a or b,
REGARDLESS OF NUMBER OF EXCESS CLUBS CARRIED:

Match play — At the conclusion of the hole at which the breach is discovered, the state of the match shall be adjusted by deducting one hole for each hole at which a breach occurred. Maximum deduction per round: two holes.

Stroke play — Two strokes for each hole at which any breach occurred; maximum penalty per round: four strokes.

Bogey and par competitions — Penalties as in match play.

Stableford competitions — See Note to Rule 32-1b.

c. Excess Club Declared Out of Play

Any club carried or used in breach of this Rule shall be declared out of play by the player immediately upon discovery that a breach has occurred and thereafter shall not be used by the player during the round.

PENALTY FOR BREACH OF RULE 4-4c: *Disqualification.*

Rule 5. The Ball

5-1. General

The ball the player uses shall conform to specifications set forth in Appendix III on maximum weight, minimum size, spherical symmetry, initial velocity and overall distance when tested under specified conditions.

5-2. Foreign Material

No foreign material shall be applied to a ball for the purpose of changing its playing characteristics.

PENALTY FOR BREACH OF RULE 5-1 or 5-2: *Disqualification.*

5-3. Ball Unfit for Play

A ball is unfit for play if it is visibly cut, cracked or out of shape. A ball is not unfit for play solely because mud or other materials adhere to it, its surface is scratched or scraped or its paint is damaged or discolored.

If a player has reason to believe his ball has become unfit for play during play of the hole being played, he may during the play of such hole lift his ball without penalty to determine whether it is unfit, provided he announces his intention in advance to his opponent in match play or his marker or a fellow-competitor in stroke play and gives his opponent, marker or fellow-competitor an opportunity to examine the ball. If he lifts the ball without announcing his intention in advance or giving his opponent, marker or fellow-competitor an opportunity to examine the ball, *he shall incur a penalty of one stroke.*

If it is determined that the ball has become unfit for play during play of the hole being played, the player may substitute another ball, placing it on the spot where the original ball lay. Otherwise, the original ball shall be replaced.

If a ball breaks into pieces as a result of a stroke, the stroke shall be replayed without penalty (see Rule 20-5).

*PENALTY FOR BREACH OF RULE 5-3:
Match play — Loss of hole; Stroke play — Two strokes.*

**If a player incurs the general penalty for breach of Rule 5-3, no additional penalty under the Rule shall be applied.*

Note 1: The ball may not be cleaned to determine whether it is unfit for play — see Rule 21.

Note 2: If the opponent, marker or fellow-competitor wishes to dispute a claim of unfitness, he must do so before the player plays another ball.

PLAYER'S RESPONSIBILITIES
Rule 6. The Player

Definition

A "marker" is one who is appointed by the Committee to record a competitor's score in stroke play. He may be a fellow-competitor. He is not a referee.

6-1. Conditions of Competition

The player is responsible for knowing the conditions under which the competition is to be played (Rule 33-1).

6-2. Handicap

a. MATCH PLAY

Before starting a match in a handicap competition, the players should determine from one another their respective handicaps. If a player begins the match having declared a higher handicap which would affect the number of strokes given or received, *he shall be disqualified*; otherwise, the player shall play off the declared handicap.

b. STROKE PLAY

In any round of a handicap competition, the competitor shall ensure that his handicap is recorded on his score card before it is returned to the Committee. If no handicap is recorded on his score card before it is returned, or if the recorded handicap is higher than that to which he is entitled and this affects the number of strokes received, *he shall be disqualified* from that round of the handicap competition; otherwise, the score shall stand.

Note: It is the player's responsibility to know the holes at which handicap strokes are to be given or received.

6-3. Time of Starting and Groups

a. TIME OF STARTING

The player shall start at the time laid down by the Committee.

b. GROUPS

In stroke play, the competitor shall remain throughout the round in the group arranged by the Committee unless the Committee authorizes or ratifies a change.

PENALTY FOR BREACH OF RULE 6-3: *Disqualification.*

(Best-ball and four-ball play — see Rules 30-3a and 31-2.)

Note: The Committee may provide in the conditions of a competition (Rule 33-1) that, if the player arrives at his starting point, ready to play, within five minutes after his starting time, in the absence of circumstances which warrant waiving the penalty of disqualification as provided in Rule 33-7, the penalty for failure to start on time is *loss of the first hole in match play or two strokes at the first hole in stroke play* instead of disqualification.

6-4. Caddie

The player may have only one caddie at any one time, *under penalty of disqualification.*

For any breach of a Rule by his caddie, the player incurs the applicable penalty.

6-5. Ball

The responsibility for playing the proper ball rests with the player. Each player should put an identification mark on his ball.

6-6. Scoring in Stroke Play

a. RECORDING SCORES

After each hole the marker should check the score with the competitor and record it. On completion of the round the marker shall sign the card and hand it to the competitor. If more than one marker records the scores, each shall sign for the part for which he is responsible.

b. SIGNING AND RETURNING CARD

After completion of the round, the competitor should check his score for each hole and settle any doubtful points with the Committee. He shall ensure that the marker has signed the card, countersign the card himself and return it to the Committee as soon as possible.

PENALTY FOR BREACH OF RULE 6-6b: *Disqualification.*

c. ALTERATION OF CARD

No alteration may be made on a card after the competitor has returned it to the Committee.

d. WRONG SCORE FOR HOLE

The competitor is responsible for the correctness of the score recorded for each hole. If he returns a score for any hole lower than actually taken, *he shall be disqualified.* If he returns a score for any hole higher than actually taken, the score as returned shall stand.

Note 1: The Committee is responsible for the addition of scores and application of the handicap recorded on the card — see Rule 33-5.

Note 2: In four-ball stroke play, see also Rule 31-4 and -7a.

6-7. Undue Delay

The player shall play without undue delay. Between completion of a hole and playing from the next teeing ground, the player shall not unduly delay play.

PENALTY FOR BREACH OF RULE 6-7:
Match play — Loss of hole; Stroke play — Two strokes.
For repeated offense — Disqualification.
If the player unduly delays play between holes, he is delaying the play of the next hole and the penalty applies to that hole.

6-8. Discontinuance of Play

a. WHEN PERMITTED

The player shall not discontinue play unless:
   (i) the Committee has suspended play;
   (ii) he believes there is danger from lightning;
   (iii) he is seeking a decision from the Committee on a doubtful or disputed point (see Rules 2-5 and 34-3); or
   (iv) there is some other good reason such as sudden illness.

Bad weather is not of itself a good reason for discontinuing play.

If the player discontinues play without specific permission from the Committee, he shall report to the Committee as soon as practicable. If he does so and the Committee considers his reason satisfactory, the player incurs no penalty. Otherwise, *the player shall be disqualified.*

Exception in match play: Players discontinuing match play by agreement are not subject to disqualification unless by so doing the competition is delayed.

Note: Leaving the course does not of itself constitute discontinuance of play.

b. PROCEDURE WHEN PLAY SUSPENDED BY COMMITTEE

When play is suspended by the Committee, if the players in a match or group are between the play of two holes, they shall not resume play until the Committee has ordered a resumption of play. If they are in the process of playing a hole, they may continue provided they do so without delay. If they choose to continue, they shall discontinue either before or immediately after completing the hole, and shall not thereafter resume play until the Committee has ordered a resumption of play.

PENALTY FOR BREACH OF RULE 6-8b: *Disqualification.*

c. LIFTING BALL WHEN PLAY DISCONTINUED

When during the play of a hole a player discontinues play under Rule 6-8a, he may lift his ball. A ball may be cleaned when so lifted. If a ball has been so lifted, the player shall, when play is resumed, place a ball on the spot from which the original ball was lifted.

PENALTY FOR BREACH OF RULE 6-8c:
Match play — Loss of hole; Stroke play — Two strokes.

Rule 7. Practice

7-1. Before or Between Rounds

a. MATCH PLAY

On any day of a match play competition, a player may practice on the competition course before a round.

b. STROKE PLAY

On any day of a stroke competition or play-off, a competitor shall not practice on the competition course or test the surface of any putting green on the course before a round or play-off. When two or more rounds of a stroke competition are to be played over consecutive days, practice between those rounds on any competition course remaining to be played is prohibited.

Exception: Practice putting or chipping on or near the first teeing ground before starting a round or play-off is permitted.

PENALTY FOR BREACH OF RULE 7-1b: *Disqualification.*

Note: The Committee may in the conditions of a competition (Rule 33-1) prohibit practice on the competition course on any day of a match play competition or permit practice on the competition course or part of the course (Rule 33-2c) on any day of or between rounds of a stroke competition.

7-2. During Round

A player shall not play a practice <u>stroke</u> either during the play of a hole or between the play of two holes except that, between the play of two holes, the player may practice putting or chipping on or near the <u>putting green</u> of the hole last played, any practice putting green or the <u>teeing ground</u> of the next hole to be played in the round, provided such practice stroke is not played from a hazard and does not unduly delay play (Rule 6-7).

Exception: When play has been suspended by the Committee, a player may, prior to resumption of play, practice (a) as provided in this Rule, (b) anywhere other than on the competition course and (c) as otherwise permitted by the Committee.

PENALTY FOR BREACH OF RULE 7-2:

Match play — Loss of hole; Stroke play — Two strokes.
In the event of a breach between the play of two holes, the penalty applies to the next hole.

Note 1: A practice swing is not a practice <u>stroke</u> and may be taken at any place, provided the player does not breach the Rules.

Note 2: The Committee may prohibit practice on or near the <u>putting green</u> of the hole last played.

Rule 8. Advice; Indicating Line of Play

Definition

"Advice" is any counsel or suggestion which could influence a player in determining his play, the choice of a club or the method of making a <u>stroke</u>.

Information on the Rules or on matters of public information, such as the position of hazards or the flagstick on the putting green, is not advice.

8-1. Advice

A player shall not give advice to anyone in the competition except his partner. A player may ask for advice from only his partner or either of their caddies.

8-2. Indicating Line of Play

a. OTHER THAN ON PUTTING GREEN

Except on the <u>putting green</u>, a player may have the line of play indicated to him by anyone, but no one shall stand on or close to the line while the <u>stroke</u> is being played. Any mark placed during the play of a hole by the player or with his knowledge to indicate the line shall be removed before the stroke is played.

Exception: Flagstick attended or held up — see Rule 17-1.

b. ON THE PUTTING GREEN

When the player's ball is on the <u>putting green</u>, the player, his partner or either of their caddies may, before but not during the <u>stroke</u>, point out a line for putting, but in so doing the putting green shall not be touched. No mark shall be placed anywhere to indicate a line for putting.

PENALTY FOR BREACH OF RULE:

Match play — Loss of hole; Stroke play — Two strokes.

Note: In a team competition without concurrent individual competition, the Committee may in the conditions of the competition (Rule 33-1) permit each team to appoint one person, *e.g.*, team captain or coach, who may give <u>advice</u> (including pointing out a line for putting) to members of that team. Such person shall be identified to the Committee prior to the start of the competition.

Rule 9. Information as to Strokes Taken

9-1. General

The number of strokes a player has taken shall include any penalty strokes incurred.

9-2. Match Play

A player who has incurred a penalty shall inform his opponent as soon as practicable. If he fails to do so, he shall be deemed to have given wrong information, even if he was not aware that he had incurred a penalty.

An opponent is entitled to ascertain from the player, during the play of a hole, the number of strokes he has taken and, after play of a hole, the number of strokes taken on the hole just completed.

If during the play of a hole the player gives or is deemed to give wrong information as to the number of strokes taken, he shall incur no penalty if he corrects the mistake before his opponent has played his next stroke. If the player fails so to correct the wrong information, *he shall lose the hole.*

If after play of a hole the player gives or is deemed to give wrong information as to the number of strokes taken on the hole just completed and this affects the opponent's understanding of the result of the hole, he shall incur no penalty if he corrects his mistake before any player plays from the next <u>teeing ground</u> or, in the case of the last hole of the match, before all players leave the <u>putting green</u>. If the player fails so to correct the wrong information, *he shall lose the hole.*

9-3. Stroke Play

A competitor who has incurred a penalty should inform his marker as soon as practicable.

ORDER OF PLAY
Rule 10. Order of Play

10-1. Match Play

a. TEEING GROUND

The side entitled to play first from the <u>teeing ground</u> is said to have the "honor."

The side which shall have the honor at the first teeing ground shall be determined by the order of the draw. In the absence of a draw, the honor should be decided by lot.

The side which wins a hole shall take the honor at the next teeing ground. If a hole has been halved, the side which had the honor at the previous teeing ground shall retain it.

b. OTHER THAN ON TEEING GROUND

When the balls are in play, the ball farther from the hole shall be played first. If the balls are equidistant from the hole, the ball to be played first should be decided by lot.

Exception: Rule 30-3c (best-ball and four-ball match play).

c. PLAYING OUT OF TURN

If a player plays when his opponent should have played, the opponent may immediately require the player to cancel the stroke so played and play a ball in correct order, without penalty (see Rule 20-5).

10-2. Stroke Play

a. TEEING GROUND

The competitor entitled to play first from the <u>teeing ground</u> is said to have the "honor."

The competitor who shall have the honor at the first teeing ground shall be determined by the order of the draw. In the absence of a draw, the honor should be decided by lot.

The competitor with the lowest score at a hole shall take the honor at the next teeing ground. The competitor with the second lowest score shall play next and so on. If two or more competitors have the same score at a hole, they shall play from the next teeing ground in the same order as at the previous teeing ground.

b. OTHER THAN ON TEEING GROUND

When the balls are in play, the ball farthest from the

hole shall be played first. If two or more balls are equidistant from the hole, the ball to be played first should be decided by lot.

Exceptions: Rules 22 (ball interfering with or assisting play) and 31-5 (four-ball stroke play).

c. PLAYING OUT OF TURN

If a competitor plays out of turn, no penalty is incurred and the ball shall be played as it lies. If, however, the Committee determines that competitors have agreed to play in an order other than that set forth in Clauses 2a and 2b of this Rule to give one of them an advantage, *they shall be disqualified.*

(Incorrect order of play in threesomes and foursomes stroke play — see Rule 29-3.)

10-3. Provisional Ball or Second Ball from Teeing Ground

If a player plays a provisional ball or a second ball from a teeing ground, he should do so after his opponent or fellow-competitor has played his first stroke. If a player plays a provisional ball or a second ball out of turn, Clauses 1c and 2c of this Rule shall apply.

10-4. Ball Moved in Measuring

If a ball is moved in measuring to determine which ball is farther from the hole, no penalty is incurred and the ball shall be replaced.

TEEING GROUND
Rule 11. Teeing Ground

Definition

The "teeing ground" is the starting place for the hole to be played. It is a rectangular area two club-lengths in depth, the front and the sides of which are defined by the outside limits of two tee-markers. A ball is outside the teeing ground when all of it lies outside the teeing ground.

11-1. Teeing

In teeing, the ball may be placed on the ground, on an irregularity of surface created by the player on the ground or on a tee, sand or other substance in order to raise it off the ground.

A player may stand outside the teeing ground to play a ball within it.

11-2. Tee-Markers

Before a player plays his first stroke with any ball from the teeing ground of the hole being played, the tee-markers are deemed to be fixed. In such circumstances, if the player moves or allows to be moved a tee-marker for the purpose of avoiding interference with his stance, the area of his intended swing or his line of play, *he shall incur the penalty for a breach of Rule 13-2.*

11-3. Ball Falling Off Tee

If a ball, when not in play, falls off a tee or is knocked off a tee by the player in addressing it, it may be re-teed without penalty, but if a stroke is made at the ball in these circumstances, whether the ball is moving or not, the stroke counts but no penalty is incurred.

11-4. Playing Outside Teeing Ground

a. MATCH PLAY

If a player, when starting a hole, plays a ball from outside the teeing ground, the opponent may immediately require the player to cancel the stroke so played and play a ball from within the teeing ground, without penalty.

b. STROKE PLAY

If a competitor, when starting a hole, plays a ball from outside the teeing ground, *he shall incur a penalty of two strokes* and shall then play a ball from within the teeing ground.

If the competitor plays a stroke from the next teeing ground without first correcting his mistake or, in the case of the last hole of the round, leaves the putting green without first declaring his intention to correct his mistake, *he shall be disqualified.*

Strokes played by a competitor from outside the teeing ground do not count in his score.

PLAYING THE BALL
Rule 12. Searching for and Identifying Ball

Definitions

A "hazard" is any bunker or water hazard.

A "bunker" is a hazard consisting of a prepared area of ground, often a hollow, from which turf or soil has been removed and replaced with sand or the like. Grass-covered ground bordering or within a bunker is not part of the bunker. The margin of a bunker extends vertically downwards, but not upwards.

A "water hazard" is any sea, lake, pond, river, ditch, surface drainage ditch or other open water course (whether or not containing water) and anything of a similar nature.

All ground or water within the margin of a water hazard is part of the water hazard. The margin of a water hazard extends vertically upwards and downwards. Stakes and lines defining the margins of water hazards are in the hazards.

12-1. Searching for Ball; Seeing Ball

In searching for his ball anywhere on the course, the player may touch or bend long grass, rushes, bushes, whins, heather or the like, but only to the extent necessary to find and identify it, provided that this does not improve the lie of the ball, the area of his intended swing or his line of play.

A player is not necessarily entitled to see his ball when playing a stroke.

In a hazard, if a ball is covered by loose impediments or sand, the player may remove by probing, raking or other means as much thereof as will enable him to see a part of the ball. If an excess is removed, no penalty is incurred and the ball shall be re-covered so that only a part of the ball is visible. If the ball is moved in such removal, no penalty is incurred; the ball shall be replaced and, if necessary, re-covered. As to removal of loose impediments outside a hazard, see Rule 23.

If a ball lying in casual water, ground under repair or a hole, cast or runway made by a burrowing animal, a reptile or a bird is accidentally moved during search, no penalty is incurred; the ball shall be replaced, unless the player elects to proceed under Rule 25-1b.

If a ball is believed to be lying in water in a water hazard, the player may probe for it with a club or otherwise. If the ball is moved in so doing, no penalty is incurred; the ball shall be replaced, unless the player elects to proceed under Rule 26-1.

PENALTY FOR BREACH OF RULE 12-1:
Match play — Loss of hole; Stroke play — Two strokes.

12-2. Identifying Ball

The responsibility for playing the proper ball rests with the player. Each player should put an identification mark on his ball.

Except in a hazard, the player may, without penalty, lift a ball he believes to be his own for the purpose of identification and clean it to the extent necessary for identification. If the ball is the player's ball, he shall replace it. Before the player lifts the ball, he shall announce his intention to his opponent in match play or his marker or a fellow-competitor in stroke play and give his opponent, marker or fellow-competitor an opportunity to observe the lifting and replacement. If he lifts his ball without announcing his intention in advance or giving his opponent, marker or fellow-competitor an opportunity to observe, or if he lifts his ball for identification in a hazard, *he shall incur a penalty of one stroke* and the ball shall be replaced.

If a player who is required to replace a ball fails to do so, *he shall incur the penalty* for a breach of Rule 20-3a, but no additional penalty under Rule 12-2 shall be applied.

Rule 13. Ball Played as It Lies; Lie, Area of Intended Swing and Line of Play; Stance

Definitions

A "hazard" is any bunker or water hazard.

A "bunker" is a hazard consisting of a prepared area of ground, often a hollow, from which turf or soil has been removed and replaced with sand or the like. Grass-covered ground bordering or within a bunker is not part of the bunker. The margin of a bunker extends vertically downwards, but not upwards.

A "water hazard" is any sea, lake, pond, river, ditch, surface drainage ditch or other open water course (whether or not containing water) and anything of a similar nature.

All ground or water within the margin of a water hazard is part of the water hazard. The margin of a water hazard extends vertically upwards and downwards. Stakes and lines defining the margins of water hazards are in the hazards.

13-1. Ball Played as It Lies

The ball shall be played as it lies, except as otherwise provided in the Rules.

(Ball at rest moved — see Rule 18.)

13-2. Improving Lie, Area of Intended Swing or Line of Play

Except as provided in the Rules, a player shall not improve or allow to be improved:

the position or lie of his ball,

the area of his intended swing,

his line of play or

the area in which he is to drop or place a ball

by any of the following actions:

moving, bending or breaking anything growing or fixed (including immovable obstructions and objects defining out of bounds) or

removing or pressing down sand, loose soil, replaced divots, other cut turf placed in position or other irregularities of surface

except as follows:

as may occur in fairly taking his stance,

in making a stroke or the backward movement of his club for a stroke,

on the teeing ground in creating or eliminating irregularities of surface, or

on the putting green in removing sand and loose soil as provided in Rule 16-1a or in repairing damage as provided in Rule 16-1c.

The club may be grounded only lightly and shall not be pressed on the ground.

Exception: Ball lying in or touching hazard — see Rule 13-4.

13-3. Building Stance

A player is entitled to place his feet firmly in taking his stance, but he shall not build a stance.

13-4. Ball Lying in or Touching Hazard

Except as provided in the Rules, before making a stroke at a ball which lies in or touches a hazard (whether a bunker or a water hazard), the player shall not:

a. Test the condition of the hazard or any similar hazard,

b. Touch the ground in the hazard or water in the water hazard with a club or otherwise, or

c. Touch or move a loose impediment lying in or touching the hazard.

Exceptions:

1. At address or in the backward movement for the stroke, the club may touch any obstruction or any grass, bush, tree or other growing thing.

2. The player may place his clubs in a hazard, provided nothing is done which may constitute testing the soil or improving the lie of the ball.

3. The player after playing the stroke, or his caddie at any time without the authority of the player, may smooth sand or soil in the hazard, provided that, if the ball still lies in the hazard, nothing is done which improves the lie of the ball or assists the player in his subsequent play of the hole.

PENALTY FOR BREACH OF RULE:
Match play — Loss of hole; Stroke play — Two strokes.

(Searching for ball — see Rule 12-1.)

Rule 14. Striking the Ball

Definition

A "stroke" is the forward movement of the club made with the intention of fairly striking at and moving the ball, but if a player checks his downswing voluntarily before the clubhead reaches the ball he is deemed not to have made a stroke.

14-1. Ball to Be Fairly Struck At

The ball shall be fairly struck at with the head of the club and must not be pushed, scraped or spooned.

14-2. Assistance

In making a stroke, a player shall not accept physical assistance or protection from the elements.

PENALTY FOR BREACH OF RULE 14-1 OR -2:
Match play — Loss of hole; Stroke play — Two strokes.

14-3. Artificial Devices and Unusual Equipment

Except as provided in the Rules, during a stipulated round the player shall not use any artificial device or unusual equipment:

a. For the purpose of gauging or measuring distance or conditions which might affect his play; or

b. Which might assist him in gripping the club, in making a stroke or in his play, except that plain gloves may be worn, resin, tape or gauze may be applied to the grip (provided such application does not render the grip non-conforming under Rule 4-1c) and a towel or handkerchief may be wrapped around the grip.

PENALTY FOR BREACH OF RULE 14-3: *Disqualification.*

14-4. Striking the Ball More than Once

If a player's club strikes the ball more than once in the course of a stroke, the player shall count the stroke and *add a penalty stroke,* making two strokes in all.

14-5. Playing Moving Ball

A player shall not play while his ball is moving.

Exceptions:

Ball falling off tee — Rule 11-3.

Striking the ball more than once — Rule 14-4.

Ball moving in water — Rule 14-6.

When the ball begins to move only after the player has begun the stroke or the backward movement of his club for the stroke, he shall incur no penalty under this Rule for playing a moving ball, but he is not exempt from any penalty incurred under the following Rules:

Ball at rest moved by player — Rule 18-2a.

Ball at rest moving after address — Rule 18-2b.

Ball at rest moving after loose impediment touched — Rule 18-2c.

14-6. Ball Moving in Water

When a ball is moving in water in a water hazard, the player may, without penalty, make a stroke, but he must not delay making his stroke in order to allow the wind or current to improve the position of the ball. A ball moving in water in a water hazard may be lifted if the player elects to invoke Rule 26.

PENALTY FOR BREACH OF RULE 14-5 or -6:
Match play — Loss of hole; Stroke play — Two strokes.

Rule 15. Playing a Wrong Ball

Definition

A "wrong ball" is any ball other than:

a. The ball in play,

b. A provisional ball or

c. In stroke play, a second ball played under Rule 3-3 or Rule 20-7b.

Note: Ball in play includes a ball substituted for the ball in play when the player is proceeding under an applicable Rule which does not permit substitution.

15-1. General

A player must hole out with the ball played from the teeing ground unless a Rule permits him to substitute another ball. If a player substitutes another ball when proceeding under an applicable Rule which does not permit substitution, that ball is not a wrong ball; it becomes the ball in play and, if the error is not corrected as provided in Rule 20-6, *the player shall incur a penalty of loss of hole in match play or two strokes in stroke play.*

15-2. Match Play

If a player plays a stroke with a <u>wrong ball</u> except in a <u>hazard</u>, *he shall lose the hole.*

If a player plays any strokes in a hazard with a wrong ball, there is no penalty. Strokes played in a hazard with a wrong ball do not count in the player's score. If the wrong ball belongs to another player, its owner shall place a ball on the spot from which the wrong ball was first played.

If the player and opponent exchange balls during the play of a hole, the first to play the wrong ball other than from a hazard shall lose the hole; when this cannot be determined, the hole shall be played out with the balls exchanged.

15-3. Stroke Play

If a competitor plays a stroke or strokes with a <u>wrong ball</u>, *he shall incur a penalty of two strokes,* unless the only stroke or strokes played with such ball were played when it was lying in a hazard, in which case no penalty is incurred.

The competitor must correct his mistake by playing the correct ball. If he fails to correct his mistake before he plays a stroke from the next <u>teeing ground</u> or, in the case of the last hole of the round, fails to declare his intention to correct his mistake before leaving the <u>putting green</u>, *he shall be disqualified.*

Strokes played by a competitor with a wrong ball do not count in his score.

If the wrong ball belongs to another competitor, its owner shall place a ball on the spot from which the wrong ball was first played.

(Lie of ball to be placed or replaced altered — see Rule 20-3b.)

THE PUTTING GREEN
Rule 16. The Putting Green

Definitions

The "putting green" is all ground of the hole being played which is specially prepared for putting or otherwise defined as such by the Committee. A ball is on the putting green when any part of it touches the putting green.

A ball is "holed" when it is at rest within the circumference of the hole and all of it is below the level of the lip of the hole.

16-1. General

a. TOUCHING LINE OF PUTT

The line of putt must not be touched except:

(i) the player may move sand and loose soil on the putting green and other <u>loose impediments</u> by picking them up or by brushing them aside with his hand or a club without pressing anything down;

(ii) in addressing the ball, the player may place the club in front of the ball without pressing anything down;

(iii) in measuring — Rule 10-4;

(iv) in lifting the ball — Rule 16-1b;

(v) in pressing down a ball-marker;

(vi) in repairing old hole plugs or ball marks on the putting green — Rule 16-1c; and

(vii) in removing movable <u>obstructions</u> — Rule 24-1.

(Indicating line for putting on putting green — see Rule 8-2b.)

b. LIFTING BALL

A ball on the <u>putting green</u> may be lifted and, if desired, cleaned. A ball so lifted shall be replaced on the spot from which it was lifted.

c. REPAIR OF HOLE PLUGS AND BALL MARKS

The player may repair an old hole plug or damage to the <u>putting green</u> caused by the impact of a ball, whether or not the player's ball lies on the putting green. If the ball is moved in the process of such repair, it shall be replaced, without penalty.

d. TESTING SURFACE

During the play of a hole, a player shall not test the surface of the <u>putting green</u> by rolling a ball or roughening or scraping the surface.

e. STANDING ASTRIDE OR ON LINE OF PUTT

The player shall not make a <u>stroke</u> on the <u>putting green</u> from a <u>stance</u> astride, or with either foot touching, the line of the putt or an extension of that line behind the ball. For the purpose of this Clause only, the line of putt does not extend beyond the hole.

f. POSITION OF CADDIE OR PARTNER

While making the <u>stroke</u>, the player shall not allow his caddie, his partner or his partner's caddie to position himself on or close to an extension of the line of putt behind the ball.

g. PLAYING STROKE WHILE ANOTHER BALL IN MOTION

A player shall not play a stroke while another ball is in motion after a stroke on the putting green.

(Lifting ball interfering with or assisting play while another ball in motion — see Rule 22.)

PENALTY FOR BREACH OF RULE 16-1:
Match play — Loss of hole; Stroke play — Two strokes.

16-2. Ball Overhanging Hole

When any part of the ball overhangs the lip of the hole, the player is allowed enough time to reach the hole without unreasonable delay and an additional ten seconds to determine whether the ball is at rest. If by then the ball has not fallen into the hole, it is deemed to be at rest. If the ball subsequently falls into the hole, the player is deemed to have holed out with his last stroke, and *he shall add a penalty stroke to his score* for the hole; otherwise there is no penalty under this Rule.

(Undue delay — see Rule 6-7.)

Rule 17. The Flagstick

17-1. Flagstick Attended, Removed or Held Up

Before and during the <u>stroke</u>, the player may have the flagstick attended, removed or held up to indicate the position of the hole. This may be done only on the authority of the player before he plays his stroke.

If the flagstick is attended, removed or held up by an opponent, a fellow-competitor or the caddie of either with the player's knowledge and no objection is made, the player shall be deemed to have authorized it. If a player or a caddie attends, removes or holds up the flagstick or stands near the hole while a stroke is being played, he shall be deemed to be attending the flagstick until the ball comes to rest.

If the flagstick is not attended before the stroke is played, it shall not be attended or removed while the ball is in motion.

17-2. Unauthorized Attendance

a. MATCH PLAY

In match play, an opponent or his caddie shall not attend, remove or hold up the flagstick without the player's knowledge or authority while the player is making a stroke or his ball is in motion.

b. STROKE PLAY

In stroke play, if a fellow-competitor or his caddie attends, removes or holds up the flagstick without the competitor's knowledge or authority while the competitor is making a stroke or his ball is in motion, *the fellow-competitor shall incur the penalty* for breach of this Rule. In such circumstances, if the competitor's ball strikes the flagstick or the person attending it, the competitor incurs no penalty and the ball shall be played as it lies, except that, if the stroke was played from the putting green, the stroke shall be replayed.

PENALTY FOR BREACH OF RULE 17-1 OR -2:
Match play — Loss of hole; Stroke play — Two strokes.

17-3. Ball Striking Flagstick or Attendant

The player's ball shall not strike:

a. The flagstick when attended, removed or held up by the player, his partner or either of their caddies, or by another person with the player's knowledge or authority; or

b. The player's caddie, his partner or his partner's caddie when attending the flagstick, or another person attending the flagstick with the player's knowledge or authority, or equipment carried by any such person; or

c. The flagstick in the hole, unattended, when the ball has been played from the putting green.

PENALTY FOR BREACH OF RULE 17-3:
Match play — Loss of hole; Stroke play — Two strokes, and the ball shall be played as it lies.

17-4. Ball Resting Against Flagstick

If the ball rests against the flagstick when it is in the hole, the player or another person authorized by him may move or remove the flagstick and if the ball falls into the hole, the player shall be deemed to have holed out at his last stroke; otherwise, the ball, if moved, shall be placed on the lip of the hole, without penalty.

BALL MOVED, DEFLECTED OR STOPPED
Rule 18. Ball at Rest Moved

Definitions

A ball is deemed to have "moved" if it leaves its position and comes to rest in any other place.

An "outside agency" is any agency not part of the match or, in stroke play, not part of a competitor's side, and includes a referee, a marker, an observer or a forecaddie. Neither wind nor water is an outside agency.

"Equipment" is anything used, worn or carried by or for the player except any ball he has played at the hole being played and any small object, such as a coin or a tee, when used to mark the position of a ball or the extent of an area in which a ball is to be dropped. Equipment includes a golf cart, whether or not motorized. If such a cart is shared by more than one player, its status under the Rules is the same as that of a caddie employed by more than one player. See "Caddie."

A player has "addressed the ball" when he has taken his stance and has also grounded his club, except that in a hazard a player has addressed the ball when he has taken his stance.

Taking the "stance" consists in a player placing his feet in position for and preparatory to making a stroke.

18-1. By Outside Agency

If a ball at rest is moved by an outside agency, the player shall incur no penalty and the ball shall be replaced before the player plays another stroke.

(Player's ball at rest moved by another ball — see Rule 18-5.)

18-2. By Player, Partner, Caddie or Equipment

a. GENERAL

When a player's ball is in play, if:

(i) the player, his partner or either of their caddies lifts or moves it, touches it purposely (except with a club in the act of addressing it) or causes it to move except as permitted by a Rule, or

(ii) equipment of the player or his partner causes the ball to move,

the player shall incur a penalty stroke. The ball shall be replaced unless the movement of the ball occurs after the player has begun his swing and he does not discontinue his swing.

Under the Rules no penalty is incurred if a player accidentally causes his ball to move in the following circumstances:

In measuring to determine which ball farther from hole — Rule 10-4

In searching for covered ball in hazard or for ball in casual water, ground under repair, etc. — Rule 12-1

In the process of repairing hole plug or ball mark — Rule 16-1c

In the process of removing loose impediment on putting green — Rule 18-2c

In the process of lifting ball under a Rule — Rule 20-1

In the process of placing or replacing ball under a Rule — Rule 20-3a

In complying with Rule 22 relating to lifting ball interfering with or assisting play

In removal of movable obstruction — Rule 24-1.

b. BALL MOVING AFTER ADDRESS

If a player's ball in play moves after he has addressed it (other than as a result of a stroke), the player shall be deemed to have moved the ball and *shall incur a penalty stroke.* The player shall replace the ball unless the movement of the ball occurs after he has begun his swing and he does not discontinue his swing.

c. BALL MOVING AFTER LOOSE IMPEDIMENT TOUCHED

Through the green, if the ball moves after any loose impediment lying within a club-length of it has been touched by the player, his partner or either of their caddies and before the player has addressed it, the player shall be deemed to have moved the ball and *shall incur a penalty stroke.* The player shall replace the ball unless the movement of the ball occurs after he has begun his swing and he does not discontinue his swing.

On the putting green, if the ball moves in the process of removing any loose impediment, it shall be replaced without penalty.

18-3. By Opponent, Caddie or Equipment in Match Play

a. DURING SEARCH

If, during search for a player's ball, it is moved by an opponent, his caddie or his equipment, no penalty is incurred and the player shall replace the ball.

b. OTHER THAN DURING SEARCH

If, other than during search for a ball, the ball is touched or moved by an opponent, his caddie or his equipment, except as otherwise provided in the Rules, *the opponent shall incur a penalty stroke.* The player shall replace the ball.

(Ball moved in measuring to determine which ball farther from the hole — see Rule 10-4.)
(Playing a wrong ball — see Rule 15-2.)
(Ball moved in complying with Rule 22 relating to lifting ball interfering with or assisting play.)

18-4. By Fellow-Competitor, Caddie or Equipment in Stroke Play

If a competitor's ball is moved by a fellow-competitor, his caddie or his equipment, no penalty is incurred. The competitor shall replace his ball.

(Playing a wrong ball — see Rule 15-3.)

18-5. By Another Ball

If a ball in play and at rest is moved by another ball in motion after a stroke, the moved ball shall be replaced.

*PENALTY FOR BREACH OF RULE:
Match play — Loss of hole; Stroke play — Two strokes.
**If a player who is required to replace a ball fails to do so, he shall incur the general penalty for breach of Rule 18 but no additional penalty under Rule 18 shall be applied.*

Note 1: If a ball to be replaced under this Rule is not immediately recoverable, another ball may be substituted.

Note 2: If it is impossible to determine the spot on which a ball is to be placed, see Rule 20-3c.

Rule 19. Ball in Motion Deflected or Stopped

Definitions

An "outside agency" is any agency not part of the match or, in stroke play, not part of a competitor's side, and includes a referee, a marker, an observer or a forecaddie. Neither wind nor water is an outside agency.

"Equipment" is anything used, worn or carried by or for the player except any ball he has played at the hole being played and any small object, such as a coin or a tee, when used to mark the position of a ball or the extent of an area in which a ball is to be dropped. Equipment includes a golf cart, whether or not motorized. If such a cart is shared by more than one player, its status under the Rules is the same as that of a caddie employed by more than one player. See "Caddie."

19-1. By Outside Agency

If a ball in motion is accidentally deflected or stopped by any <u>outside agency</u>, it is a <u>rub of the green</u>, no penalty is incurred and the ball shall be played as it lies except:

a. If a ball in motion after a <u>stroke</u> other than on the <u>putting green</u> comes to rest in or on any moving or animate outside agency, the player shall, <u>through the green</u> or in a <u>hazard</u>, drop the ball, or on the putting green place the ball, as near as possible to the spot where the outside agency was when the ball came to rest in or on it, and

b. If a ball in motion after a stroke on the putting green is deflected or stopped by, or comes to rest in or on, any moving or animate outside agency except a worm or an insect, the stroke shall be cancelled and the ball shall be replaced.

If the ball is not immediately recoverable, another ball may be substituted.

(Player's ball deflected or stopped by another ball — see Rule 19-5.)

Note: If the referee or the Committee determines that a competitor's ball has been purposely deflected or stopped by an <u>outside agency</u>, Rule 1-4 applies to the competitor. If the outside agency is a fellow-competitor or his caddie, Rule 1-2 applies to the fellow-competitor.

19-2. By Player, Partner, Caddie or Equipment

a. MATCH PLAY

If a player's ball is accidentally deflected or stopped by himself, his partner or either of their caddies or <u>equipment</u>, *he shall lose the hole.*

b. STROKE PLAY

If a competitor's ball is accidentally deflected or stopped by himself, his partner or either of their caddies or <u>equipment</u>, *the competitor shall incur a penalty of two strokes.* The ball shall be played as it lies, except when it comes to rest in or on the competitor's, his partner's or either of their caddies' clothes or equipment, in which case the competitor shall <u>through the green</u> or in a <u>hazard</u> drop the ball, or on the <u>putting green</u> place the ball, as near as possible to where the article was when the ball came to rest in or on it.

Exception: Dropped ball — see Rule 20-2a.

(Ball purposely deflected or stopped by player, partner or caddie — see Rule 1-2.)

19-3. By Opponent, Caddie or Equipment in Match Play

If a player's ball is accidentally deflected or stopped by an opponent, his caddie or his <u>equipment</u>, no penalty is incurred. The player may play the ball as it lies or, before another <u>stroke</u> is played by either side, cancel the stroke and replay it (see Rule 20-5). If the player elects to replay the stroke and the original ball is not immediately recoverable, another ball may be substituted.

If the ball has come to rest in or on the opponent's or his caddie's clothes or equipment, the player may <u>through the green</u> or in a <u>hazard</u> drop the ball, or on the putting green place the ball, as near as possible to where the article was when the ball came to rest in or on it.

Exception: Ball striking person attending flagstick — see Rule 17-3b.

(Ball purposely deflected or stopped by opponent or caddie — see Rule 1-2.)

19-4. By Fellow-Competitor, Caddie or Equipment in Stroke Play

See Rule 19-1 regarding ball deflected by outside agency.

19-5. By Another Ball

If a player's ball in motion after a stroke is deflected or stopped by a ball at rest, the player shall play his ball as it lies. In stroke play, if both balls lay on the <u>putting green</u> prior to the stroke, *the player incurs a penalty of two strokes.* Otherwise, no penalty is incurred.

If a player's ball in motion after a stroke is deflected or stopped by another ball in motion, the player shall play his ball as it lies. There is no penalty unless the player was in breach of Rule 16-1g, in which case *he shall incur the penalty for breach of that Rule.*

Exception: Ball in motion after a stroke on the putting green deflected or stopped by moving or animate outside agency — see Rule 19-1b.

PENALTY FOR BREACH OF RULE:
Match play — Loss of hole; Stroke play — Two strokes.

RELIEF SITUATIONS AND PROCEDURE
Rule 20. Lifting, Dropping and Placing; Playing from Wrong Place

20-1. Lifting

A ball to be lifted under the Rules may be lifted by the player, his partner or another person authorized by the player. In any such case, the player shall be responsible for any breach of the Rules.

The position of the ball shall be marked before it is lifted under a Rule which requires it to be replaced. If it is not marked, the player *shall incur a penalty of one stroke* and the ball shall be replaced. If it is not replaced, *the player shall incur the general penalty* for breach of this Rule but no additional penalty under Rule 20-1 shall be applied.

If a ball or a ball-marker is accidentally moved in the process of lifting the ball under a Rule or marking its position, no penalty is incurred and the ball or the ball-marker shall be replaced.

Note: The position of a ball to be lifted should be marked by placing a ball-marker, a small coin or other similar object immediately behind the ball. If the ball-marker interferes with the play, <u>stance</u> or <u>stroke</u> of another player, it should be placed one or more clubhead-lengths to one side.

20-2. Dropping and Re-dropping

a. BY WHOM AND HOW

A ball to be dropped under the Rules shall be dropped by the player himself. He shall stand erect, hold the ball at shoulder height and arm's length and drop it. If a ball is dropped by any other person or in any other manner and the error is not corrected as provided in Rule 20-6, *the player shall incur a penalty stroke.*

If the ball touches the player, his partner, either of their caddies or their equipment before or after it strikes the ground, the ball shall be re-dropped, without penalty. There is no limit to the number of times a ball shall be re-dropped in such circumstances.

(Taking action to influence position or movement of ball — see Rule 1-2.)

b. WHERE TO DROP

When a ball is to be dropped, it shall be dropped as near as possible to the spot where the ball lay, but not nearer the hole, except when a Rule permits or requires it to be dropped elsewhere. If a ball is to be dropped in a <u>hazard</u>, the ball shall be dropped in and come to rest in that hazard.

Note: A ball when dropped must first strike the ground where the applicable Rule requires it to be dropped. If it is not so dropped, Rules 20-6 and -7 apply.

c. WHEN TO RE-DROP

A dropped ball shall be re-dropped without penalty if it:
    (i) rolls into a <u>hazard</u>;
    (ii) rolls out of a hazard;
    (iii) rolls onto a <u>putting green</u>;
    (iv) rolls <u>out of bounds</u>;
    (v) rolls back into the condition from which relief was taken under Rule 24-2 (immovable obstruction) or Rule 25 (abnormal ground conditions and wrong putting green);
    (vi) rolls and comes to rest more than two club-lengths from where it first struck the ground; or
    (vii) rolls and comes to rest nearer the hole than its original position unless otherwise permitted by the Rules.

If the ball again rolls into such position, it shall be placed as near as possible to the spot where it first struck the ground when re-dropped.

If a ball to be re-dropped or placed under this Rule is not immediately recoverable, another ball may be substituted.

20-3. Placing and Replacing

a. BY WHOM AND WHERE

A ball to be placed under the Rules shall be placed by the player or his partner. A ball to be replaced shall be replaced by the player, his partner or the person who lifted or moved it. In any such case, the player shall be responsible for any breach of the Rules.

If a ball or a ball-marker is accidentally moved in the process of placing or replacing the ball, no penalty is incurred and the ball or the ball-marker shall be replaced.

b. LIE OF BALL TO BE PLACED OR REPLACED ALTERED

If the original lie of a ball to be placed or replaced has been altered:

(i) except in a hazard, the ball shall be placed in the nearest lie most similar to the original lie which is not more than one club-length from the original lie, not nearer the hole and not in a hazard;

(ii) in a water hazard, the ball shall be placed in accordance with Clause (i) above, except that the ball must be placed in the water hazard;

(iii) in a bunker, the original lie shall be recreated as nearly as possible and the ball shall be placed in that lie.

c. SPOT NOT DETERMINABLE

If it is impossible to determine the spot where the ball is to be placed:

(i) through the green, the ball shall be dropped as near as possible to the place where it lay but not nearer the hole or in a hazard;

(ii) in a hazard, the ball shall be dropped in the hazard as near as possible to the place where it lay but not nearer the hole;

(iii) on the putting green, the ball shall be placed as near as possible to the place where it lay but not nearer the hole or in a hazard.

d. BALL FAILS TO REMAIN ON SPOT

If a ball when placed fails to remain on the spot on which it was placed, it shall be replaced without penalty. If it still fails to remain on that spot:

(i) except in a hazard, it shall be placed at the nearest spot not nearer the hole or in a hazard where it can be placed at rest;

(ii) in a hazard, it shall be placed in the hazard at the nearest spot not nearer the hole where it can be placed at rest.

PENALTY FOR BREACH OF RULE 20-1, -2 or -3:
Match play — Loss of hole; Stroke play — Two strokes.

20-4. When Ball Dropped or Placed Is in Play

If the player's ball in play has been lifted, it is again in play when dropped or placed.

A substituted ball becomes the ball in play if it is dropped or placed under an applicable Rule, whether or not such Rule permits substitution. A ball substituted under an inapplicable Rule is a wrong ball.

20-5. Playing Next Stroke from Where Previous Stroke Played

When, under the Rules, a player elects or is required to play his next stroke from where a previous stroke was played, he shall proceed as follows: If the stroke is to be played from the teeing ground, the ball to be played shall be played from anywhere within the teeing ground and may be teed; if the stroke is to be played from through the green or a hazard, it shall be dropped; if the stroke is to be played on the putting green, it shall be placed.

PENALTY FOR BREACH OF RULE 20-5:
Match play — Loss of hole; Stroke play — Two strokes.

20-6. Lifting Ball Wrongly Dropped or Placed

A ball dropped or placed in a wrong place or otherwise not in accordance with the Rules but not played may be lifted, without penalty, and the player shall then proceed correctly.

20-7. Playing from Wrong Place

For a ball played outside teeing ground, see Rule 11-4.

a. MATCH PLAY

If a player plays a stroke with a ball which has been dropped or placed in a wrong place, *he shall lose the hole.*

b. STROKE PLAY

If a competitor plays a stroke with (i) his original ball which has been dropped or placed in a wrong place, (ii) a substituted ball which has been dropped or placed under an applicable Rule but in a wrong place or (iii) his ball in play when it has been moved and not replaced in a case where the Rules require replacement, *he shall*, provided a serious breach has not occurred, *incur the penalty prescribed by the applicable Rule* and play out the hole with the ball.

If, after playing from a wrong place, a competitor becomes aware of that fact and believes that a serious breach may be involved, he may, provided he has not played a stroke from the next teeing ground or, in the case of the last hole of the round, left the putting green, declare that he will play out the hole with a second ball dropped or placed in accordance with the Rules. The competitor shall report the facts to the Committee before returning his score card; if he fails to do so, *he shall be disqualified.* The Committee shall determine whether a serious breach of the Rule occurred. If so, the score with the second ball shall count and *the competitor shall add two penalty strokes to his score with that ball.*

If a serious breach has occurred and the competitor has failed to correct it as prescribed above, *he shall be disqualified.*

Note: If a competitor plays a second ball, penalty strokes incurred by playing the ball ruled not to count and strokes subsequently taken with that ball shall be disregarded.

Rule 21. Cleaning Ball

A ball on the putting green may be cleaned when lifted under Rule 16-1b. Elsewhere, a ball may be cleaned when lifted except when it has been lifted:

a. To determine if it is unfit for play (Rule 5-3);

b. For identification (Rule 12-2), in which case it may be cleaned only to the extent necessary for identification; or

c. Because it is interfering with or assisting play (Rule 22).

If a player cleans his ball during play of a hole except as provided in this Rule, *he shall incur a penalty of one stroke* and the ball, if lifted, shall be replaced.

If a player who is required to replace a ball fails to do so, *he shall incur the penalty* for breach of Rule 20-3a, but no additional penalty under Rule 21 shall be applied.

Exception: If a player incurs a penalty for failing to act in accordance with Rule 5-3, 12-2 or 22, no additional penalty under Rule 21 shall be applied.

Rule 22. Ball Interfering with or Assisting Play

Any player may:

a. Lift his ball if he considers that it might assist any other player or

b. Have any other ball lifted if he considers that it might interfere with his play or assist the play of any other player,

but this may not be done while another ball is in motion. In stroke play, a player required to lift his ball may play first rather than lift. A ball lifted under this Rule shall be replaced.

If a ball is accidentally moved in complying with this Rule, no penalty is incurred and the ball shall be replaced.

PENALTY FOR BREACH OF RULE:
Match play — Loss of hole; Stroke play — Two strokes.

Rule 23. Loose Impediments

Definition

"Loose impediments" are natural objects such as stones, leaves, twigs, branches and the like, dung, worms and insects and casts or heaps made by them, provided they are not fixed or growing, are not solidly embedded and do not adhere to the ball.

Sand and loose soil are loose impediments on the putting green but not elsewhere.

Snow and ice are either casual water or loose impediments, at the option of the player, except that manufactured ice is an obstruction.

Dew is not a loose impediment.

23-1. Relief

Except when both the loose impediment and the ball lie in or touch a hazard, any loose impediment may be removed without penalty. If the ball moves, see Rule 18-2c.

When a player's ball is in motion, a loose impediment on his line of play shall not be removed.

PENALTY FOR BREACH OF RULE:
Match play — Loss of hole; Stroke play — Two strokes.

(Searching for ball in hazard — see Rule 12-1.)
(Touching line of putt — see Rule 16-1a.)

Rule 24. Obstructions

Definition

An "obstruction" is anything artificial, including the artificial surfaces and sides of roads and paths and manufactured ice, except:

a. Objects defining out of bounds, such as walls, fences, stakes and railings;

b. Any part of an immovable artificial object which is out of bounds; and

c. Any construction declared by the Committee to be an integral part of the course.

24-1. Movable Obstruction

A player may obtain relief from a movable obstruction as follows:

a. If the ball does not lie in or on the obstruction, the obstruction may be removed; if the ball moves, no penalty is incurred and the ball shall be replaced.

b. If the ball lies in or on the obstruction, the ball may be lifted, without penalty, and the obstruction removed. The ball shall through the green or in a hazard be dropped, or on the putting green be placed, as near as possible to the spot directly under the place where the ball lay in or on the obstruction, but not nearer the hole.

The ball may be cleaned when lifted under Rule 24-1.

When a ball is in motion, an obstruction on the player's line of play other than an attended flagstick and equipment of the players shall not be removed.

24-2. Immovable Obstruction

a. INTERFERENCE

Interference by an immovable obstruction occurs when a ball lies in or on the obstruction, or so close to the obstruction that the obstruction interferes with the player's stance or the area of his intended swing. If the player's ball lies on the putting green, interference also occurs if an immovable obstruction on the putting green intervenes on his line of putt. Otherwise, intervention on the line of play is not, of itself, interference under this Rule.

b. RELIEF

Except when the ball lies in or touches a water hazard or a lateral water hazard, a player may obtain relief from interference by an immovable obstruction, without penalty, as follows:

(i) *Through the Green:* If the ball lies through the green, the point on the course nearest to where the ball lies shall be determined (without crossing over, through or under the obstruction) which (a) is not nearer the hole, (b) avoids interference (as defined) and (c) is not in a hazard or on a putting green. The player shall lift the ball and drop it within one club-length of the point thus determined on ground which fulfils (a), (b) and (c) above.

Note: The prohibition against crossing over, through or under the obstruction does not apply to the artificial surfaces and sides of roads and paths or when the ball lies in or on the obstruction.

(ii) *In a Bunker:* If the ball lies in or touches a bunker, the player shall lift and drop the ball in accordance with Clause (i) above, except that the ball must be dropped in the bunker.

(iii) *On the Putting Green:* If the ball lies on the putting green, the player shall lift the ball and place it in the nearest position to where it lay which affords relief from interference, but not nearer the hole nor in a hazard.

The ball may be cleaned when lifted under Rule 24-2b.

(Ball rolling back into condition from which relief taken — see Rule 20-2c(v).)

Exception: A player may not obtain relief under Rule 24-2b if (a) it is clearly unreasonable for him to play a stroke because of interference by anything other than an immovable obstruction or (b) interference by an immovable obstruction would occur only through use of an unnecessarily abnormal stance, swing or direction of play.

Note: If a ball lies in or touches a water hazard (including a lateral water hazard), the player is not entitled to relief without penalty from interference by an immovable obstruction. The player shall play the ball as it lies or proceed under Rule 26-1.

PENALTY FOR BREACH OF RULE:
Match play — Loss of hole; Stroke play — Two strokes.

Rule 25. Abnormal Ground Conditions and Wrong Putting Green

Definitions

"Casual water" is any temporary accumulation of water on the course which is visible before or after the player takes his stance and is not in a water hazard. Snow and ice are either casual water or loose impediments, at the option of the player, except that manufactured ice is an obstruction. Dew is not casual water.

"Ground under repair" is any portion of the course so marked by order of the Committee or so declared by its authorized representative. It includes material piled for removal and a hole made by a greenkeeper, even if not so marked. Stakes and lines defining ground under repair are in such ground. The margin of ground under repair extends vertically downwards, but not upwards.

Note 1: Grass cuttings and other material left on the course which have been abandoned and are not intended to be removed are not ground under repair unless so marked.

Note 2: The Committee may make a Local Rule prohibiting play from ground under repair.

25-1. Casual Water, Ground Under Repair and Certain Damage to Course

a. INTERFERENCE

Interference by casual water, ground under repair or a hole, cast or runway made by a burrowing animal, a reptile or a bird occurs when a ball lies in or touches any of these conditions or when the condition interferes with the player's stance or the area of his intended swing.

If the player's ball lies on the putting green, interference also occurs if such condition on the putting green intervenes on his line of putt.

If interference exists, the player may either play the ball as it lies (unless prohibited by Local Rule) or take relief as provided in Clause b.

b. RELIEF

If the player elects to take relief, he shall proceed as follows:

(i) *Through the Green:* If the ball lies through the green, the point on the course nearest to where the ball lies shall be determined which (a) is not nearer the hole, (b) avoids interference by the condition, and (c) is not in a hazard or on a putting green. The player shall lift the ball and drop it without penalty within one club-length of the point thus determined on ground which fulfils (a), (b) and (c) above.

(ii) *In a Hazard:* If the ball lies in or touches a hazard, the player shall lift and drop the ball either:

(a) Without penalty, in the hazard, as near as possible to the spot where the ball lay, but not nearer the hole, on ground which affords maximum available relief from the condition;

or

(b) *Under penalty of one stroke,* outside the hazard, keeping the point where the ball lay directly between the hole and the spot on which the ball is dropped.

Exception: If a ball lies in or touches a water hazard (including a lateral water hazard), the player is not entitled to relief without penalty from a hole, cast or runway made by a burrowing animal, a reptile or a bird. The player shall play the ball as it lies or proceed under Rule 26-1.

(iii) *On the Putting Green:* If the ball lies on the putting green, the player shall lift the ball and place it without penalty in the nearest position to where it lay which affords maximum available relief from the condition, but not nearer the hole nor in a hazard.

The ball may be cleaned when lifted under Rule 25-1b.

(Ball rolling back into condition from which relief taken — see Rule 20-2c(v).)

Exception: A player may not obtain relief under Rule 25-1b if (a) it is clearly unreasonable for him to play a stroke because of interference by anything other than a condition covered by Rule 25-1a or (b) interference by such a condition would occur only through use of an unnecessarily abnormal stance, swing or direction of play.

c. BALL LOST UNDER CONDITION COVERED BY RULE 25-1

It is a question of fact whether a ball lost after having been struck toward a condition covered by Rule 25-1 is lost under such condition. In order to treat the ball as lost under such condition, there must be reasonable evidence to that effect. In the absence of such evidence, the ball must be treated as a lost ball and Rule 27 applies.

(i) *Outside a Hazard* — If a ball is lost outside a hazard under a condition covered by Rule 25-1, the player may take relief as follows: the point on the course nearest to where the ball last crossed the margin of the area shall be determined which (a) is not nearer the hole than where the ball last crossed the margin, (b) avoids interference by the condition and (c) is not in a hazard or on a putting green. He shall drop a ball without penalty within one club-length of the point thus determined on ground which fulfils (a), (b) and (c) above.

(ii) *In a Hazard* — If a ball is lost in a hazard under a condition covered by Rule 25-1, the player may drop a ball either:

(a) Without penalty, in the hazard, as near as possible to the point at which the original ball last crossed the margin of the area, but not nearer the hole, on ground which affords maximum available relief from the condition

or

(b) *Under penalty of one stroke,* outside the hazard, keeping the point at which the original ball last crossed the margin of the hazard directly between the hole and the spot on which the ball is dropped.

Exception: If a ball lies in a water hazard (including a lateral water hazard), the player is not entitled to relief without penalty for a ball lost in a hole, cast or runway made by a burrowing animal, a reptile or a bird. The player shall proceed under Rule 26-1.

25-2. Embedded Ball

A ball embedded in its own pitch-mark in the ground in any closely mown area through the green may be lifted, cleaned and dropped, without penalty, as near as possible to the spot where it lay but not nearer the hole. "Closely mown area" means any area of the course, including paths through the rough, cut to fairway height or less.

25-3. Wrong Putting Green

If a ball lies on a putting green other than that of the hole being played, the point on the course nearest to where the ball lies shall be determined which (a) is not nearer the hole and (b) is not in a hazard or on a putting green. The player shall lift the ball and drop it without penalty within one club-length of the point thus determined on ground which fulfils (a) and (b) above. The ball may be cleaned when so lifted.

Note: Unless otherwise prescribed by the Committee, the term "a putting green other than that of the hole being played" includes a practice putting green or pitching green on the course.

PENALTY FOR BREACH OF RULE:
Match play — Loss of hole; Stroke play — Two strokes.

Rule 26. Water Hazards (Including Lateral Water Hazards)

Definitions

A "water hazard" is any sea, lake, pond, river, ditch, surface drainage ditch or other open water course (whether or not containing water) and anything of a similar nature.

All ground or water within the margin of a water hazard is part of the water hazard. The margin of a water hazard extends vertically upwards and downwards. Stakes and lines defining the margins of water hazards are in the hazards.

Note: Water hazards (other than lateral water hazards) should be defined by yellow stakes or lines.

A "lateral water hazard" is a water hazard or that part of a water hazard so situated that it is not possible or is deemed by the Committee to be impracticable to drop a ball behind the water hazard in accordance with Rule 26-1b.

That part of a water hazard to be played as a lateral water hazard should be distinctively marked.

Note: Lateral water hazards should be defined by red stakes or lines.

26-1. Ball in Water Hazard

It is a question of fact whether a ball lost after having been struck toward a water hazard is lost inside or outside the hazard. In order to treat the ball as lost in the hazard, there must be reasonable evidence that the ball lodged in it. In the absence of such evidence, the ball must be treated as a lost ball and Rule 27 applies.

If a ball lies in, touches or is lost in a water hazard (whether the ball lies in water or not), the player may *under penalty of one stroke:*

a. Play his next stroke as nearly as possible at the spot from which the original ball was last played (see Rule 20-5);

or

b. Drop a ball behind the water hazard, keeping the point at which the original ball last crossed the margin of the water hazard directly between the hole and the spot on which the ball is dropped, with no limit to how far behind the water hazard the ball may be dropped.

or

c. *As additional options available only if the ball lies in, touches or is lost in a lateral water hazard,* drop a ball outside the water hazard within two club-lengths of (i) the point where the original ball last crossed the margin of the water hazard or (ii) a point on the opposite margin of the water hazard equidistant from the hole. The ball must be dropped and come to rest not nearer the hole than the point where the original ball last crossed the margin of the water hazard.

The ball may be cleaned when lifted under this Rule.

(Ball moving in water in a water hazard — see Rule 14-6.)

26-2. Ball Played Within Water Hazard

a. BALL COMES TO REST IN HAZARD

If a ball played from within a water hazard comes to rest in the hazard after the stroke, the player may:

(i) proceed under Rule 26-1; or

(ii) *under penalty of one stroke,* play his next stroke as nearly as possible at the spot from which the last stroke from outside the hazard was played (see Rule 20-5).

b. BALL LOST OR UNPLAYABLE OUTSIDE HAZARD OR OUT OF BOUNDS

If a ball played from within a water hazard is lost or declared unplayable outside the hazard or is out of bounds, the player, after taking *a penalty of one stroke* under Rule 27-1 or 28a, may:

(i) play a ball as nearly as possible at the spot in the hazard from which the original ball was last played (see Rule 20-5); or

(ii) *under an additional penalty of one stroke,* proceed under Rule 26-1b or, if applicable, Rule 26-1c, using as the reference point the point where the original ball last crossed the margin of the hazard before it came to rest in the hazard; or

(iii) *under an additional penalty of one stroke,* play his next stroke as nearly as possible at the spot from which the last stroke from outside the hazard was played (see Rule 20-5).

Note: If a ball played from within a water hazard is declared unplayable outside the hazard, nothing in Rule 26-2b precludes the player from proceeding under Rule 28b or c.

PENALTY FOR BREACH OF RULE:
Match play — Loss of hole; Stroke play — Two strokes.

Rule 27. Ball Lost or Out of Bounds; Provisional Ball

If the original ball is lost under a condition covered by Rule 25-1 (casual water, ground under repair and certain damage to the course), the player may proceed under that Rule. If the original ball is lost in a water hazard, the player shall proceed under Rule 26.

Such Rules may not be used unless there is reasonable evidence that the ball is lost under a condition covered by Rule 25-1 or in a water hazard.

Definitions

A ball is "lost" if:

a. It is not found or identified as his by the player within five minutes after the player's side or his or their caddies have begun to search for it; or

b. The player has put another ball into play under the Rules, even though he may not have searched for the original ball; or

c. The player has played any stroke with a provisional ball from the place where the original ball is likely to be or from a point nearer the hole than that place, whereupon the provisional ball becomes the ball in play.

Time spent in playing a wrong ball is not counted in the five-minute period allowed for search.

"Out of bounds" is ground on which play is prohibited.

When out of bounds is defined by reference to stakes or a fence, or as being beyond stakes or a fence, the out of bounds line is determined by the nearest inside points of the stakes or fence posts at ground level excluding angled supports.

When out of bounds is defined by a line on the ground, the line itself is out of bounds.

The out of bounds line extends vertically upwards and downwards.

A ball is out of bounds when all of it lies out of bounds.

A player may stand out of bounds to play a ball lying within bounds.

A "provisional ball" is a ball played under Rule 27-2 for a ball which may be lost outside a water hazard or may be out of bounds.

27-1. Ball Lost or Out of Bounds

If a ball is lost outside a water hazard or is out of bounds, the player shall play a ball, *under penalty of one stroke,* as nearly as possible at the spot from which the original ball was last played (see Rule 20-5).

PENALTY FOR BREACH OF RULE 27-1:
Match play — Loss of hole; Stroke play — Two strokes.

27-2. Provisional Ball

a. PROCEDURE

If a ball may be lost outside a water hazard or may be out of bounds, to save time the player may play another ball provisionally as nearly as possible at the spot from which the original ball was played (see Rule 20-5). The player shall inform his opponent in match play or his marker or a fellow-competitor in stroke play that he intends to play a provisional ball, and he shall play it before he or his partner goes forward to search for the original ball. If he fails to do so and plays another ball, such ball is not a provisional ball and becomes the ball in play *under penalty of stroke and distance* (Rule 27-1); the original ball is deemed to be lost.

b. WHEN PROVISIONAL BALL BECOMES BALL IN PLAY

The player may play a provisional ball until he reaches the place where the original ball is likely to be. If he plays a stroke with the provisional ball from the place where the original ball is likely to be or from a point nearer the hole than that place, the original ball is deemed to be lost and the provisional ball becomes the ball in play *under penalty of stroke and distance* (Rule 27-1).

If the original ball is lost outside a water hazard or is out of bounds, the provisional ball becomes the ball in play, *under penalty of stroke and distance* (Rule 27-1).

c. WHEN PROVISIONAL BALL TO BE ABANDONED

If the original ball is neither lost outside a water hazard nor out of bounds, the player shall abandon the provisional ball and continue play with the original ball. If he fails to do so, any further strokes played with the provisional ball shall constitute playing a wrong ball and the provisions of Rule 15 shall apply.

Note: If the original ball lies in a water hazard, the player shall play the ball as it lies or proceed under Rule 26. If it is lost in a water hazard or unplayable, the player shall proceed under Rule 26 or 28, whichever is applicable.

Rule 28. Ball Unplayable

The player may declare his ball unplayable at any place on the course except when the ball lies in or touches a water hazard. The player is the sole judge as to whether his ball is unplayable.

If the player deems his ball to be unplayable, he shall, *under penalty of one stroke:*

a. Play his next stroke as nearly as possible at the spot from which the original ball was last played (see Rule 20-5);

or

b. Drop a ball within two club-lengths of the spot where the ball lay, but not nearer the hole;

or

c. Drop a ball behind the point where the ball lay, keeping that point directly between the hole and the spot on which the ball is dropped, with no limit to how far behind that point the ball may be dropped.

If the unplayable ball lies in a bunker and the player elects to proceed under Clause b or c, a ball must be dropped in the bunker.

The ball may be cleaned when lifted under this Rule.

PENALTY FOR BREACH OF RULE:
Match play — Loss of hole; Stroke play — Two strokes.

OTHER FORMS OF PLAY
Rule 29. Threesomes and Foursomes

Definitions

Threesome: A match in which one plays against two, and each side plays one ball.

Foursome: A match in which two play against two, and each side plays one ball.

29-1. General

In a threesome or a foursome, during any stipulated round the partners shall play alternately from the teeing grounds and alternately during the play of each hole. Penalty strokes do not affect the order of play.

29-2. Match Play

If a player plays when his partner should have played, *his side shall lose the hole.*

29-3. Stroke Play

If the partners play a stroke or strokes in incorrect order, such stroke or strokes shall be cancelled and *the side shall incur a penalty of two strokes.* The side shall correct the error by playing a ball in correct order at the spot from which it first played in incorrect order (see Rule 20-5). If the side plays a stroke from the next <u>teeing ground</u> without first correcting the error or, in the case of the last hole of the round, leaves the <u>putting green</u> without declaring its intention to correct the error, *the side shall be disqualified.*

Rule 30. Three-Ball, Best-Ball and Four-Ball Match Play

Definitions

Three-Ball: A match play competition in which three play against one another, each playing his own ball. Each player is playing two distinct matches.

Best-Ball: A match in which one plays against the better ball of two or the best ball of three players.

Four-Ball: A match in which two play their better ball against the better ball of two other players.

30-1. Rules of Golf Apply

The Rules of Golf, so far as they are not at variance with the following special Rules, shall apply to three-ball, best-ball and four-ball matches.

30-2. Three-Ball Match Play

a. BALL AT REST MOVED BY AN OPPONENT

Except as otherwise provided in the Rules, if the player's ball is touched or moved by an opponent, his <u>caddie</u> or <u>equipment</u> other than during search, Rule 18-3b applies. *That opponent shall incur a penalty stroke in his match with the player,* but not in his match with the other opponent.

b. BALL DEFLECTED OR STOPPED BY AN OPPONENT ACCIDENTALLY

If a player's ball is accidentally deflected or stopped by an opponent, his <u>caddie</u> or <u>equipment</u>, no penalty shall be incurred. In his match with that opponent the player may play the ball as it lies or, before another stroke is played by either side, he may cancel the stroke and replay it (see Rule 20-5). In his match with the other opponent, the ball shall be played as it lies.

Exception: Ball striking person attending flagstick — see Rule 17-3b.

(Ball purposely deflected or stopped by opponent — see Rule 1-2.)

30-3. Best-Ball and Four-Ball Match Play

a. REPRESENTATION OF SIDE

A side may be represented by one partner for all or any part of a match; all partners need not be present. An absent partner may join a match between holes, but not during play of a hole.

b. MAXIMUM OF FOURTEEN CLUBS

The side shall be penalized for a breach of Rule 4-4 by any partner.

c. ORDER OF PLAY

Balls belonging to the same side may be played in the order the side considers best.

d. WRONG BALL

If a player plays a stroke with a <u>wrong ball</u> except in a <u>hazard</u>, *he shall be disqualified for that hole,* but his partner incurs no penalty even if the wrong ball belongs to him. The owner of the ball shall replace it on the spot from which it was played, without penalty. If the ball is not immediately recoverable, another ball may be substituted.

e. DISQUALIFICATION OF SIDE

(i) *A side shall be disqualified* for a breach of any of the following by any partner:

 Rule 1-3 — Agreement to Waive Rules.
 Rule 4-1, -2 or -3 — Clubs.
 Rule 5-1 or -2 — The Ball.
 Rule 6-2a — Handicap (playing off higher handicap).
 Rule 6-4 — Caddie.
 Rule 6-7 — Undue Delay (repeated offense).
 Rule 14-3 — Artificial Devices and Unusual Equipment.

(ii) *A side shall be disqualified* for a breach of any of the following by all partners:

 Rule 6-3 — Time of Starting and Groups.
 Rule 6-8 — Discontinuance of Play.

f. EFFECT OF OTHER PENALTIES

If a player's breach of a Rule assists his partner's play or adversely affects an opponent's play, *the partner incurs the applicable penalty in addition to any penalty incurred by the player.*

In all other cases where a player incurs a penalty for breach of a Rule, the penalty shall not apply to his partner. Where the penalty is stated to be loss of hole, the effect shall be to disqualify the player for that hole.

g. ANOTHER FORM OF MATCH PLAYED CONCURRENTLY

In a best-ball or four-ball match when another form of match is played concurrently, the above special Rules shall apply.

Rule 31. Four-Ball Stroke Play

In four-ball stroke play two competitors play as partners, each playing his own ball. The lower score of the partners is the score for the hole. If one partner fails to complete the play of a hole, there is no penalty.

31-1. Rules of Golf Apply

The Rules of Golf, so far as they are not at variance with the following special Rules, shall apply to four-ball stroke play.

31-2. Representation of Side

A side may be represented by either partner for all or any part of a <u>stipulated round</u>; both partners need not be present. An absent competitor may join his partner between holes, but not during play of a hole.

31-3. Maximum of Fourteen Clubs

The side shall be penalized for a breach of Rule 4-4 by either partner.

31-4. Scoring

The marker is required to record for each hole only the gross score of whichever partner's score is to count. The gross scores to count must be individually identifiable; otherwise *the side shall be disqualified.* Only one of the partners need be responsible for complying with Rule 6-6b.

(Wrong score — see Rule 31-7a.)

31-5. Order of Play

Balls belonging to the same side may be played in the order the side considers best.

31-6. Wrong Ball

If a competitor plays a stroke with a <u>wrong ball</u> except in a <u>hazard</u>, *he shall add two penalty strokes to his score for the hole* and shall then play the correct ball. His partner incurs no penalty even if the wrong ball belongs to him.

The owner of the ball shall replace it on the spot from which it was played, without penalty. If the ball is not immediately recoverable, another ball may be substituted.

31-7. Disqualification Penalties

a. BREACH BY ONE PARTNER

A side shall be disqualified from the competition for a breach of any of the following by either partner:

 Rule 1-3 — Agreement to Waive Rules.
 Rule 3-4 — Refusal to Comply with Rule.
 Rule 4-1, -2 or -3 — Clubs.
 Rule 5-1 or -2 — The Ball.
 Rule 6-2b — Handicap (playing off higher handicap;

failure to record handicap).

Rule 6-4 — Caddie.

Rule 6-6b — Signing and Returning Card.

Rule 6-6d — Wrong Score for Hole, *i.e.*, when the recorded lower score of the partners is lower than actually taken. If the recorded lower score of the partners is higher than actually taken, it must stand as returned.

Rule 6-7 — Undue Delay (repeated offense).

Rule 7-1 — Practice Before or Between Rounds.

Rule 14-3 — Artificial Devices and Unusual Equipment.

Rule 31-4 — Gross Scores to Count Not Individually Identifiable.

b. Breach by Both Partners

A side shall be disqualified:

(i) for a breach by both partners of Rule 6-3 (Time of Starting and Groups) or Rule 6-8 (Discontinuance of Play), or

(ii) if, at the same hole, each partner is in breach of a Rule the penalty for which is disqualification from the competition or for a hole.

c. For the Hole Only

In all other cases where a breach of a Rule would entail disqualification, *the competitor shall be disqualified only for the hole at which the breach occurred.*

31-8. Effect of Other Penalties

If a competitor's breach of a Rule assists his partner's play, *the partner incurs the applicable penalty in addition to any penalty incurred by the competitor.*

In all other cases where a competitor incurs a penalty for breach of a Rule, the penalty shall not apply to his partner.

Rule 32. Bogey, Par and Stableford Competitions

32-1. Conditions

Bogey, par and Stableford competitions are forms of stroke competition in which play is against a fixed score at each hole. The Rules for stroke play, so far as they are not at variance with the following special Rules, apply.

a. Bogey and Par Competitions

The reckoning for bogey and par competitions is made as in match play. Any hole for which a competitor makes no return shall be regarded as a loss. The winner is the competitor who is most successful in the aggregate of holes.

The marker is responsible for marking only the gross number of strokes for each hole where the competitor makes a net score equal to or less than the fixed score.

Note: Maximum of 14 clubs — Penalties as in match play — see Rule 4-4.

b. Stableford Competitions

The reckoning in Stableford competitions is made by points awarded in relation to a fixed score at each hole as follows:

Hole Played In	Points
More than one over fixed score or no score returned	0
One over fixed score	1
Fixed score	2
One under fixed score	3
Two under fixed score	4
Three under fixed score	5

The winner is the competitor who scores the highest number of points.

The marker shall be responsible for marking only the gross number of strokes at each hole where the competitor's net score earns one or more points.

Note: Maximum of 14 clubs (Rule 4-4) — Penalties applied as follows: From total points scored for the round, deduction of two points for each hole at which any breach occurred; maximum deduction per round: four points.

32-2. Disqualification Penalties

a. From the Competition

A competitor shall be disqualified from the competition for a breach of any of the following:

Rule 1-3 — Agreement to Waive Rules.

Rule 3-4 — Refusal to Comply with Rule.

Rule 4-1, -2 or -3 — Clubs.

Rule 5-1 or -2 — The Ball.

Rule 6-2b — Handicap (playing off higher handicap; failure to record handicap).

Rule 6-3 — Time of Starting and Groups.

Rule 6-4 — Caddie.

Rule 6-6b — Signing and Returning Card.

Rule 6-6d — Wrong Score for Hole, except that no penalty shall be incurred when a breach of this Rule does not affect the result of the hole.

Rule 6-7 — Undue Delay (repeated offense).

Rule 6-8 — Discontinuance of Play.

Rule 7-1 — Practice Before or Between Rounds.

Rule 14-3 — Artificial Devices and Unusual Equipment.

b. For a Hole

In all other cases where a breach of a Rule would entail disqualification, *the competitor shall be disqualified only for the hole at which the breach occurred.*

ADMINISTRATION
Rule 33. The Committee

33-1. Conditions: Waiving Rule

The Committee shall lay down the conditions under which a competition is to be played.

The Committee has no power to waive a Rule of Golf.

Certain special rules governing stroke play are so substantially different from those governing match play that combining the two forms of play is not practicable and is not permitted. The results of matches played and the scores returned in these circumstances shall not be accepted.

In stroke play the Committee may limit a referee's duties.

33-2. The Course

a. Defining Bounds and Margins

The Committee shall define accurately:

(i) the course and out of bounds,

(ii) the margins of water hazards and lateral water hazards,

(iii) ground under repair, and

(iv) obstructions and integral parts of the course.

b. New Holes

New holes should be made on the day on which a stroke competition begins and at such other times as the Committee considers necessary, provided all competitors in a single round play with each hole cut in the same position.

Exception: When it is impossible for a damaged hole to be repaired so that it conforms with the Definition, the Committee may make a new hole in a nearby similar position.

c. Practice Ground

Where there is no practice ground available outside the area of a competition course, the Committee should lay down the area on which players may practice on any day of a competition, if it is practicable to do so. On any day of a stroke competition, the Committee should not normally permit practice on or to a putting green or from a hazard of the competition course.

d. Course Unplayable

If the Committee or its authorized representative considers that for any reason the course is not in a playable condition or that there are circumstances which render the proper playing of the game impossible, it may, in match play or stroke play, order a temporary suspension of play or, in stroke play, declare play null and void and cancel all scores for the round in question. When play has been temporarily suspended, it shall be resumed from where it was discontinued, even though resumption occurs on a subsequent day. When a round is cancelled, all penalties incurred in that round are cancelled.

(Procedure in discontinuing play — see Rule 6-8.)

33-3. Times of Starting and Groups

The Committee shall lay down the times of starting and, in stroke play, arrange the groups in which competitors shall play.

When a match play competition is played over an extended period, the Committee shall lay down the limit of time within which each round shall be completed. When players are allowed to arrange the date of their match within these limits, the Committee should announce that the match must be played at a stated time on the last day of the period unless the players agree to a prior date.

33-4. Handicap Stroke Table

The Committee shall publish a table indicating the order of holes at which handicap strokes are to be given or received.

33-5. Score Card

In stroke play, the Committee shall issue for each competitor a score card containing the date and the competitor's name or, in foursome or four-ball stroke play, the competitors' names.

In stroke play, the Committee is responsible for the addition of scores and application of the handicap recorded on the card.

In four-ball stroke play, the Committee is responsible for recording the better-ball score for each hole and in the process applying the handicaps recorded on the card, and adding the better-ball scores.

In bogey, par and Stableford competitions, the Committee is responsible for applying the handicap recorded on the card and determining the result of each hole and the overall result or points total.

33-6. Decision of Ties

The Committee shall announce the manner, day and time for the decision of a halved match or of a tie, whether played on level terms or under handicap.

A halved match shall not be decided by stroke play. A tie in stroke play shall not be decided by a match.

33-7. Disqualification Penalty; Committee Discretion

A penalty of disqualification may in exceptional individual cases be waived, modified or imposed if the Committee considers such action warranted.

33-8. Local Rules

a. POLICY

The Committee may make and publish Local Rules for abnormal conditions if they are consistent with the policy of the Governing Authority for the country concerned as set forth in Appendix I to these Rules.

b. WAIVING PENALTY

A penalty imposed by a Rule of Golf shall not be waived by a Local Rule.

Rule 34. Disputes and Decisions

34-1. Claims and Penalties

a. MATCH PLAY

In match play if a claim is lodged with the Committee under Rule 2-5, a decision should be given as soon as possible so that the state of the match may, if necessary, be adjusted.

If a claim is not made within the time limit provided by Rule 2-5, it shall not be considered unless it is based on facts previously unknown to the player making the claim and the player making the claim had been given wrong information (Rules 6-2a and 9) by an opponent. In any case, no later claim shall be considered after the result of the match has been officially announced, unless the Committee is satisfied that the opponent knew he was giving wrong information.

b. STROKE PLAY

Except as provided below, in stroke play no penalty shall be rescinded, modified or imposed after the com-

petition is closed. A competition is deemed to have closed when the result has been officially announced or, in stroke play qualifying followed by match play, when the player has teed off in his first match.

A penalty of disqualification shall be imposed at any time if a competitor:

(i) returns a score for any hole lower than actually taken (Rule 6-6d) for any reason other than failure to include a penalty which he did not know he had incurred; or

(ii) returns a score card on which he has recorded a handicap which he knows is higher than that to which he is entitled, and this affects the number of strokes received (Rule 6-2b).

34-2. Referee's Decision

If a referee has been appointed by the Committee, his decision shall be final.

34-3. Committee's Decision

In the absence of a referee, the players shall refer any dispute to the Committee, whose decision shall be final.

If the Committee cannot come to a decision, it shall refer the dispute to the Rules of Golf Committee of the United States Golf Association, whose decision shall be final.

If the point in doubt or dispute has not been referred to the Rules of Golf Committee, the player or players have the right to refer an agreed statement through the Secretary of the Club to the Rules of Golf Committee for an opinion as to the correctness of the decision given. The reply will be sent to the Secretary of the Club or Clubs concerned.

If play is conducted other than in accordance with the Rules of Golf, the Rules of Golf Committee will not give a decision on any question.

Appendix I
LOCAL RULES

Rule 33-8 provides:

"The Committee may make and publish Local Rules for abnormal conditions if they are consistent with the policy of the Governing Authority for the country concerned as set forth in Appendix I to these Rules.

"A penalty imposed by a Rule of Golf shall not be waived by a Local Rule."

Among the matters for which Local Rules may be advisable are the following:

1. Obstructions

Clarifying the status of objects which may be obstructions (Rule 24).

Declaring any construction to be an integral part of the course and, accordingly, not an obstruction, *e.g.*, built-up sides of teeing grounds, putting greens and bunkers (Rules 24 and 33-2a).

2. Roads and Paths

Providing relief of the type afforded under Rule 24-2b from roads and paths not having artificial surfaces and sides if they could unfairly affect play.

3. Preservation of Course

Preservation of the course by defining areas, including turf nurseries and other parts of the course under cultivation, as ground under repair from which play is prohibited.

4. Unusual Damage to the Course

(other than as covered in Rule 25)

5. Water Hazards

Lateral Water Hazards. Clarifying the status of sections of water hazards which may be lateral water hazards (Rule 26).

Provisional Ball. Permitting play of a provisional ball for a ball which may be in a water hazard of such character that it would be impracticable to determine whether the ball is in the hazard or to do so would unduly delay play. In such case, if a provisional ball is played and the original ball is in a water hazard, the player may play the original ball as it lies or continue the provisional ball in play, but he may not proceed under Rule 26-1.

6. Defining Bounds and Margins

Specifying means used to define out of bounds, hazards, water hazards, lateral water hazards and ground under repair.

7. Ball Drops

Establishment of special areas on which balls may be dropped when it is not feasible or practicable to proceed exactly in conformity with Rule 24-2b (immovable obstructions), Rule 25-1b or -1c (ground under repair), Rule 26-1 (water hazards and lateral water hazards) and Rule 28 (ball unplayable).

8. Temporary Conditions — Mud, Extreme Wetness

Temporary conditions which might interfere with proper playing of the game, including mud and extreme wetness warranting lifting an embedded ball anywhere through the green (see detailed recommendation below) or removal of mud from a ball through the green.

Lifting an Embedded Ball

Rule 25-2 provides relief without penalty for a ball embedded in its own pitch-mark in any closely mown area through the green.

On the putting green, a ball may be lifted and damage caused by the impact of a ball may be repaired (Rules 16-1b and c).

When permission to lift an embedded ball anywhere through the green would be warranted, the following Local Rule is suggested:

Anywhere "through the green," a ball which is embedded in its own pitch-mark in the ground, except in loose sand, may be lifted without penalty, cleaned and dropped as near as possible to the spot where it lay but not nearer the hole. (See Rule 20.)

("Through the green" is the whole area of the course except:

a. Teeing ground and putting green of the hole being played;

b. All hazards on the course.)

Practice Between Holes

When, between the play of two holes, it is desired to prohibit practice putting or chipping on or near the putting green of the hole last played, the following Local Rule is recommended:

Between the play of two holes, a player shall not play any practice stroke on or near the putting green of the hole last played. (For other practice, see Rules 7 and 33-2c.)

PENALTY FOR BREACH OF LOCAL RULE:
Match play — Loss of next hole; Stroke play — Two strokes at next hole.

Marking Position of Lifted Ball

When it is desired to require a specific means of marking the position of a lifted ball on the putting green, the following Local Rule is recommended:

Before a ball on the putting green is lifted, its position shall be marked by placing a small coin or some similar object immediately behind the ball; if the ball-marker interferes with another player, it should be moved one or more putterhead-lengths to one side. If the position of the ball is not so marked, *the player shall incur a penalty of one stroke* and the ball shall be replaced. If the ball is not replaced, *the player shall incur the penalty* for breach of Rule 20-3a, but no additional penalty under this Local Rule shall be applied. (This modifies Rule 20-1.)

Prohibition Against Touching Line of Putt with Club

When it is desired to prohibit touching the line of putt with a club in moving loose impediments, the following Local Rule is recommended:

The line of putt shall not be touched with a club for any purpose except to repair old hole plugs or ball marks or during address. (This modifies Rule 16-1a.)

PENALTY FOR BREACH OF LOCAL RULE:
Match play — Loss of hole; Stroke play — Two strokes.

Temporary Obstructions

When temporary obstructions are installed for a competition, the following Local Rule is recommended:

1. Definition

Temporary immovable obstructions include tents, scoreboards, grandstands, refreshment stands, lavatories and, provided it is not mobile or otherwise readily movable, any temporary equipment for photography, press, radio and television.

Excluded are temporary power lines and cables and mats covering them and temporary telephone lines and stanchions supporting them (from which relief is provided in Clause 5) and mobile or otherwise readily movable equipment for photography, press, radio or television (from which relief is obtainable under Rule 24-1).

2. Interference

Interference by a temporary immovable obstruction occurs when (a) the ball lies in or on the obstruction or so close to the obstruction that the obstruction interferes with the player's stance or the area of his intended swing or (b) the obstruction intervenes between the player's ball and the hole or the ball lies within one club-length of a spot where such intervention would exist.

3. Relief

A player may obtain relief from interference by a temporary immovable obstruction as follows:

a. THROUGH THE GREEN

Through the green, the point on the course nearest to where the ball lies shall be determined which (a) is not nearer the hole, (b) avoids interference as defined in Clause 2 of this Local Rule and (c) is not in a hazard or on a putting green. He shall lift the ball and drop it without penalty within one club-length of the point thus determined on ground which fulfils (a), (b) and (c) above. The ball may be cleaned when so lifted.

b. IN A HAZARD

If the ball lies in a hazard, the player shall lift and drop the ball either:

(i) in the hazard, without penalty, on the nearest ground affording complete relief within the limits specified in Clause 3a above or, if complete relief is impossible, on ground within the hazard affording maximum relief, or

(ii) outside the hazard, *under penalty of one stroke*, as follows: The player shall determine the point on the course nearest to where the ball lies which (a) is not nearer the hole, (b) avoids interference as defined in Clause 2 of this Local Rule and (c) is not in a hazard. He shall drop the ball within one club-length of the point thus determined on ground which fulfils (a), (b) and (c) above.

The ball may be cleaned when so lifted.

Exception: A player may not obtain relief under Clause 3a or 3b if (a) it is clearly unreasonable for him to play a stroke, or in the case of intervention to play a stroke toward the hole, because of interference by anything other than a temporary immovable obstruction or (b) interference by a temporary immovable obstruction would occur only through use of an unnecessarily abnormal stance, swing or direction of play.

4. Ball Lost in Temporary Immovable Obstruction

If there is reasonable evidence that a ball is lost within the confines of a temporary immovable obstruction, the player may take relief without penalty as prescribed in Rule 25-1c.

5. Temporary Power Lines and Cables

The above Clauses do not apply to (1) temporary power lines or cables or mats covering them or (2) temporary telephone lines or stanchions supporting them. If such items are readily movable, the player may obtain relief under Rule 24-1. If they are not readily movable, the player may, if the ball lies through the green, obtain relief as provided in Rule 24-2b(i). If the ball lies in a bunker or a water hazard, the player may obtain relief under Rule 24-2b(i), except that the ball must be dropped in the bunker or water hazard.

Note: The prohibition in Rule 24-2b(i) against crossing over, through or under the obstruction does not apply.

If a ball strikes a temporary power line or cable which is elevated, it must be replayed, without penalty (see Rule 20-5). If the ball is not immediately recoverable, another ball may be substituted.

Exception: Ball striking elevated junction section of cable rising from the ground shall not be replayed.

6. Re-Dropping

If a dropped ball rolls into a position covered by this Local Rule, or nearer the hole than its original position, it shall be re-dropped without penalty. If it again rolls into such a position, it shall be placed where it first struck the ground when re-dropped.

PENALTY FOR BREACH OF LOCAL RULE:
Match play — Loss of hole; Stroke play — Two strokes.

"Preferred Lies" and "Winter Rules"

The USGA does not endorse "preferred lies" and "winter rules" and recommends that the Rules of Golf be observed uniformly. Ground under repair is provided for in Rule 25. Occasional abnormal conditions which might interfere with fair play and are not widespread should be defined accurately as ground under repair.

However, adverse conditions are sometimes so general throughout a course that the Committee believes "preferred lies" or "winter rules" would promote fair play or help protect the course. Heavy snows, spring thaws, prolonged rains or extreme heat can make fairways unsatisfactory and sometimes prevent use of heavy mowing equipment.

When a Committee adopts a Local Rule for "preferred lies" or "winter rules," it should be in detail and should be interpreted by the Committee, as there is no established code for "winter rules." Without a detailed Local Rule, it is meaningless for a Committee to post a notice merely saying "Winter Rules Today."

The following Local Rule would seem appropriate for the conditions in question, but the USGA will not interpret it:

A ball lying on a "fairway" may be lifted and cleaned, without penalty, and placed within six inches of where it originally lay, not nearer the hole, and so as to preserve as nearly as possible the stance required to play from the original lie. After the ball has been so placed, it is in play, and if it moves after the player has addressed it, *the penalty shall be one stroke* — see Rule 18-2b.

If the adverse conditions extend onto the putting green, the above Local Rule may be altered by adding the words "or the putting green" after the word "fairway."

The above Local Rule does not require a player to move his ball if he does not want to do so. If it is desired to *protect* the course, the above Local Rule should be reworded to make it mandatory rather than permissive to move the ball from certain areas.

Before a Committee adopts a Local Rule permitting "preferred lies" or "winter rules," the following facts should be considered:

1. Such a Local Rule conflicts with the Rules of Golf and the fundamental principle of playing the ball as it lies.

2. "Winter rules" are sometimes adopted under the guise of protecting the course when, in fact, the practical effect is just the opposite — they permit moving the ball to the best turf, from which divots are then taken to injure the course further.

3. "Preferred lies" or "winter rules" tend generally to lower scores and handicaps, thus penalizing the players

in competition with players whose scores for handicaps are made under the Rules of Golf.

4. Extended use or indiscriminate use of "preferred lies" or "winter rules" will place players at a disadvantage when competing at a course where the ball must be played as it lies.

Handicapping and "Preferred Lies"

Scores made under a Local Rule for "preferred lies" or "winter rules" may be accepted for handicapping if the Committee considers that conditions warrant.

When such a Local Rule is adopted, the Committee should ensure that the course's normal scoring difficulty is maintained as nearly as possible through adjustment of tee-markers and related methods. However, if extreme conditions cause extended use of "preferred lies" or "winter rules" and the course management cannot adjust scoring difficulty properly, the club should obtain a Temporary Course Rating from its district golf association.

Appendices II and III

Any design in a club or ball which is not covered by Rules 4 and 5 and Appendices II and III, or which might significantly change the nature of the game, will be ruled on by the United States Golf Association and the Royal and Ancient Golf Club of St. Andrews.

Note: Equipment approved for use or marketed prior to January 1, 1984 which conformed to the Rules in effect in 1983 but does not conform to the 1984 Rules may be used until December 31, 1989; thereafter all equipment must conform to the current Rules.

Appendix II
DESIGN OF CLUBS

Rule 4-1 prescribes general regulations for the design of clubs. The following paragraphs, which provide some detailed specifications and clarify how Rule 4-1 is interpreted, should be read in conjunction with this Rule.

4-1b. Shaft

GENERALLY STRAIGHT
The shaft shall be at least 18 inches (457mm) in length. It shall be straight from the top of the grip to a point not more than 5 inches (127mm) above the sole, measured along the axis of the shaft and the neck or socket.

BENDING AND TWISTING PROPERTIES
The shaft must be so designed and manufactured that at any point along its length:
(i) it bends in such a way that the deflection is the same regardless of how the shaft is rotated about its longitudinal axis; and
(ii) it twists the same amount in both directions.

ATTACHMENT TO CLUBHEAD
The neck or socket must not be more than 5 inches (127mm) in length, measured from the top of the neck or socket to the sole along its axis. The shaft and the neck or socket must remain in line with the heel, or with a point to the right or left of the heel, when the club is viewed in the address position. The distance between the axis of the shaft or the neck or socket and the back of the heel must not exceed 0.625 inches (16mm).

Exception for Putters: The shaft or neck or socket of a putter may be fixed at any point in the head and need not remain in line with the heel. The axis of the shaft from the top to a point not more than 5 inches (127mm) above the sole must diverge from the vertical in the toe-heel plane by at least 10 degrees when the club is in its normal address position.

4-1c. Grip

(i) For clubs other than putters the grip must be generally circular in cross-section, except that a continuous, straight, slightly raised rib may be incorporated along the full length of the grip.
(ii) A putter grip may have a non-circular cross-section, provided the cross-section has no concavity and remains generally similar throughout the length of the grip.

(iii) The grip may be tapered but must not have any bulge or waist.

(iv) For clubs other than putters the axis of the grip must coincide with the axis of the shaft.

4-1d. Clubhead

DIMENSIONS

The dimensions of a clubhead (see diagram) are measured, with the clubhead in its normal address position, on horizontal lines between vertical projections of the outermost points of (i) the heel and the toe and (ii) the face and the back. If the outermost point of the heel is not clearly defined, it is deemed to be 0.625 inches (16mm) above the horizontal plane on which the club is resting in its normal address position.

PLAIN IN SHAPE

The clubhead shall be generally plain in shape. All parts shall be rigid, structural in nature and functional.

Features such as holes through the head, windows or transparencies, or appendages to the main body of the head such as plates, rods or fins for the purpose of meeting dimensional specifications, for aiming or for any other purpose are not permitted. Exceptions may be made for putters.

Any furrows in or runners on the sole shall not extend into the face.

4-1e. Club Face

HARDNESS AND RIGIDITY

The club face must not be designed and manufactured to have the effect at impact of a spring which would unduly influence the movement of the ball.

MARKINGS

Except for specified markings, the surface roughness must not exceed that of decorative sandblasting. Markings must not have sharp edges or raised lips, as determined by a finger test. Markings within the area where impact is intended (the "impact area") are governed by the following:

(i) *Grooves.* A series of straight grooves with diverging sides and a symmetrical cross-section may be used. (See diagram.) The width and cross-section must be generally consistent across the face of the club and along the length of the grooves. Any rounding of groove edges shall be in the form of a radius which does not exceed 0.020 inches (0.5mm). The width of the grooves shall not exceed 0.035 inches (0.9mm), using the 30 degree method of measurement on file with the United States Golf Association. The distance between edges of adjacent grooves must not be less than three times the width of a groove, and not less than 0.075 inches (1.9mm). The depth of a groove must not exceed 0.020 inches (0.5mm).

(ii) *Punch Marks.* Punch marks may be used. The area of any such mark must not exceed 0.0044 square inches (2.8 sq. mm). A mark must not be closer to an adjacent mark than 0.168 inches (4.3mm), measured from center to center. The depth of a punch mark must not exceed 0.040 inches (1.0mm). If punch marks are used in combination with grooves, a punch mark may not be closer to a groove than 0.168 inches (4.3mm), measured from center to center.

DECORATIVE MARKINGS

The center of the impact area may be indicated by a design within the boundary of a square whose sides are 0.375 inches (9.5mm) in length. Such a design must not unduly influence the movement of the ball. Markings outside the impact area must not be greater than 0.040 inches (1.0mm) in depth and width.

NON-METALLIC CLUB FACE MARKINGS

The above specifications for markings do not apply to non-metallic clubs with loft angles less than 24 degrees, but markings which could unduly influence the movement of the ball are prohibited. Non-metallic clubs with a loft or face angle exceeding 24 degrees may have grooves of maximum width 0.040 inches (1.0mm) and maximum depth 1½ times the groove width, but must otherwise conform to the markings specifications above.

CLUBS

GRIPS

CLUB GRIP CIRCULAR

PUTTER GRIP FLAT SIDE (Permitted on Putters only)

GROOVES

Groove width max. 0.035"

Groove depth max. 0.020"

EXAMPLES OF PERMISSIBLE GROOVE CROSS-SECTIONS

Appendix III
THE BALL

a. WEIGHT

The weight of the ball shall not be greater than 1.620 ounces avoirdupois (45.93gm).

b. SIZE

The diameter of the ball shall be not less than 1.680 inches (42.67mm). This specification will be satisfied if, under its own weight, a ball falls through a 1.680 inches diameter ring gauge in fewer than 25 out of 100 randomly selected positions, the test being carried out at a temperature of $23\pm1°C$.

c. SPHERICAL SYMMETRY

The ball shall be designed and manufactured to perform in general as if it were spherically symmetrical.

As outlined in procedures on file at the United States Golf Association, differences in peak angle of trajectory, carry and time of flight will be measured when 40 balls of the same type are launched, spinning 20 about one axis and 20 about another axis.

These tests will be performed using apparatus approved by the United States Golf Association. If in two successive tests differences in the same two or more measurements are statistically significant at the 5% level of significance and exceed the limits set forth below, the ball type will not conform to the symmetry specification.

MEASUREMENT	MAXIMUM ABSOLUTE DIFFERENCE OF THE MEANS
Peak angle of trajectory	0.9 grid units (approx. 0.4 degrees)
Carry distance	2.5 yards
Flight time	0.16 seconds

Note: Methods of determining whether a ball performs as if it were generally spherically symmetrical may be subject to change as instrumentation becomes available to measure other properties accurately, such as the aerodynamic coefficient of lift, coefficient of drag and moment of inertia.

d. Initial Velocity

The velocity of the ball shall not be greater than 250 feet (76.2m) per second when measured on apparatus approved by the United States Golf Association. A maximum tolerance of 2% will be allowed. The temperature of the ball when tested shall be 23±1°C.

e. Overall Distance Standard

A brand of golf ball, when tested on apparatus approved by the USGA on the outdoor range at the USGA Headquarters under the conditions set forth in the Overall Distance Standard for golf balls on file with the USGA, shall not cover an average distance in carry and roll exceeding 280 yards plus a tolerance of 6%. *Note:* The 6% tolerance will be reduced to a minimum of 4% as test techniques are improved.

Exception: In international team competitions, the size of the ball shall not be less than 1.620 inches (41.15 mm) in diameter and the Overall Distance Standard shall not apply if the diameter of the ball is less than 1.680 inches (42.67mm).

Note: The Rules of the Royal and Ancient Golf Club of St. Andrews provide for the same specifications as those set forth above except that the size of the ball must not be less than 1.620 inches (41.15 mm) in diameter and there is no Overall Distance Standard.

Appendix IV
MISCELLANEOUS

Fundamentals of the USGA Handicap System

General

The USGA Handicap System is designed to provide equitable handicaps for golfers throughout the United States.

A USGA Handicap is determined by multiplying by 96% the average of the lowest 10 handicap differentials of the last 20 scores. A handicap differential is the score minus the Course Rating, except another step is involved if the Slope System is being used. A player who has returned between 5 and 19 scores is eligible for a USGA Handicap, but in such cases fewer than 10 scores are used to determine his handicap. USGA Handicaps must be revised no less often than once a month and no more often than once every two weeks. Only a golf club or a golf association can be authorized to issue USGA Handicaps.

In areas not using the Slope System, a player plays off his USGA Handicap, which is expressed as a whole number.

In areas using the Slope System, each player is issued a USGA Handicap Index, which is expressed in strokes and decimal fractions of a stroke. A player's USGA Handicap Index is converted through use of a Course Handicap Table to a Course Handicap, and he plays off the Course Handicap.

Following are some fundamental aspects of the USGA Handicap System.

Scores to Be Used

The USGA Handicap System is based on the assumption that every player will endeavor to make the best score he can in every round he plays and that he will report every eligible score, good and bad, for handicap purposes, regardless of where the round is played. Eligible scores are those made in 18-hole rounds or those obtained by combining consecutive nine-hole scores. If a player plays 13 or more holes but does not complete the round, he must also record a score, using for the incompleted holes the total of par for those holes, plus any handicap strokes he would receive on those holes. Scores must be made under the Rules of Golf. Scores in both match and stroke play shall be used.

Scores Not to Be Used

A score is not acceptable for handicap purposes if made:

a. When less than 13 holes are played, except that consecutive nine-hole scores shall be used.

b. When the types of clubs are limited (as in competitions in which only iron clubs are allowed).

c. When the length of the course is less than 3,000 yards if the Slope System is used or less than 5,000 yards (4,000 for women) if the Slope System is not used.

d. In an area in which an inactive season established by the governing golf association is in effect.

Equitable Stroke Control (ESC)

a. A score for any hole is reduced to a specified number of strokes over par for handicap purposes only, as follows:

Handicap	Limitation on Hole Score
Plus or scratch	Limit of one over par on any hole.
1 through 18	Limit of two over par on number of holes equal to handicap. Limit of one over par on balance of holes.
19 through 36	Limit of three over par on as many holes as the handicap exceeds 18 strokes. Limit of two over par on balance of holes.
37 through 40	Limit of four over par on as many holes as the handicap exceeds 36 strokes. Limit of three over par on balance of holes.

b. Reduction of hole scores for handicap purposes only in accordance with the above formula is called "Equitable Stroke Control" or ESC. Each player is responsible for adjusting his score in accordance with the ESC formula before it is returned for handicap purposes. This is done by adding the number of strokes taken in excess of the formula on any hole and deducting the total from the gross score.

Player Belonging to More Than One Club

If a player belongs to more than one club, he may either (a) designate one club as the authority for his handicap and return to that club all scores made at all his clubs, (b) return all scores to all his clubs or (c) register as a multi-member with the computer center, if such service is provided, so that all scores at every club will enter into his handicap computation.

This will result in the same handicap at every club unless there are different revision dates. If a player has different handicaps because of different revision dates, he shall use his lowest handicap when competing with players from more than one club.

Players Competing from Different Sets of Tees

When players competing against one another are playing from different sets of tees, the player playing from the set of tees from which the Course Rating is higher shall receive additional handicap strokes equal to the difference between the two Course Ratings. The same applies if a man and woman compete from the same set of tees. Decimals are rounded off to the nearest whole number, with a decimal of .5 being rounded upward. *Example:* If a woman playing from the forward or red tees from which the women's Course Rating is 73.5 competes against a man playing from the middle tees from which the men's Course Rating is 70.9, the woman shall add three strokes (73.5 − 70.9 = 2.6 or 3 strokes) to her handicap.

Recommended Handicap Allowances

Singles match play: Allow the higher-handicapped player the full difference between the handicaps of the two players.

Four-ball match play: Reduce the handicaps of all four players by the handicap of the low-handicapped player, who shall then play from scratch. Allow each of the three other players 100 percent of the resulting difference.

Individual stroke play: Allow the full handicap.

Four-ball stroke play: Men — Allow each competitor 90 percent of his handicap. Women — Allow each competitor 95 percent of her handicap.

Best-ball-of-four, stroke play: Men — Allow each competitor 80 percent of his handicap. Women — Allow each competitor 90 percent of her handicap.

Note: Except in individual stroke play, a player receives

his handicap strokes in the order assigned on the score card. In individual stroke play, the full handicap is deducted from the total score.

Details of the USGA Handicap System are contained in the booklet "USGA Handicap System and Golf Committee Manual," available from Golf House.

How to Decide Ties

Rule 33-6 empowers the Committee to determine how and when a halved match or a stroke play tie shall be decided. The decision should be published in advance.

The USGA recommends:

1. Match Play

A match which ends all square should be played off hole by hole until one side wins a hole. The play-off should start on the hole where the match began. In a handicap match, handicap strokes should be allowed as in the prescribed round.

2. Stroke Play

(a) In the event of a tie in a scratch stroke play competition, an 18-hole play-off is recommended. If that is not feasible, a sudden-death play-off is recommended.

(b) In the event of a tie in a handicap stroke play competition, a play-off over 18 holes with handicaps is recommended. If a shorter play-off is necessary, the percentage of 18 holes to be played should be applied to the players' handicaps to determine their play-off handicaps. It is advisable to arrange for a percentage of holes that will result in whole numbers in handicaps; if this is not feasible, handicap stroke fractions of one-half stroke or more should count as a full stroke and any lesser fraction should be disregarded.

(c) In either a scratch or handicap stroke play competition, if a play-off of any type is not feasible, matching score cards is recommended. The method of matching cards should be announced in advance. An acceptable method of matching cards is to determine the winner on the basis of the best score for the last nine holes. If the tying players have the same score for the last nine, determine the winner on the basis of the last six holes, last three holes and finally the 18th hole. If such a method is used in a handicap stroke play competition, one-half, one-third, one-sixth, etc. of the handicaps should be deducted.

(d) If the conditions of the competition provide that ties shall be decided over the last nine, last six, last three and last hole, they should also provide what will happen if this procedure does not produce a winner.

Pairings for Match Play

General Numerical Draw

For purposes of determining places in the draw, ties in qualifying rounds other than those for the last qualifying place shall be decided by the order in which scores are returned, the first score to be returned receiving the lowest available number, etc. If it is impossible to determine the order in which scores are returned, ties shall be determined by a blind draw.

Upper Half	Lower Half	Upper Half	Lower Half
64 Qualifiers		32 Qualifiers	
1 vs. 64	2 vs. 63	1 vs. 32	2 vs. 31
32 vs. 33	31 vs. 34	16 vs. 17	15 vs. 18
16 vs. 49	15 vs. 50	8 vs. 25	7 vs. 26
17 vs. 48	18 vs. 47	9 vs. 24	10 vs. 23
8 vs. 57	7 vs. 58	4 vs. 29	3 vs. 30
25 vs. 40	26 vs. 39	13 vs. 20	14 vs. 19
9 vs. 56	10 vs. 55	5 vs. 28	6 vs. 27
24 vs. 41	23 vs. 42	12 vs. 21	11 vs. 22
4 vs. 61	3 vs. 62	16 Qualifiers	
29 vs. 36	30 vs. 35	1 vs. 16	2 vs. 15
13 vs. 52	14 vs. 51	8 vs. 9	7 vs. 10
20 vs. 45	19 vs. 46	4 vs. 13	3 vs. 14
5 vs. 60	6 vs. 59	5 vs. 12	6 vs. 11
28 vs. 37	27 vs. 38	8 Qualifiers	
12 vs. 53	11 vs. 54	1 vs. 8	2 vs. 7
21 vs. 44	22 vs. 43	4 vs. 5	3 vs. 6

Par Computation

"Par" is the score that an expert golfer would be expected to make for a given hole. Par means errorless play without flukes and under ordinary weather conditions, allowing two strokes on the putting green.

Yardages for guidance in computing par are given below. They should not be applied arbitrarily; allowance should be made for the configuration of the ground, any difficult or unusual conditions and the severity of the hazards.

Each hole should be measured horizontally from the middle of the tee area to be used to the center of the green, following the line of play planned by the architect in laying out the hole. Thus, in a hole with a bend, the line at the elbow point should be centered in the fairway in accordance with the architect's intention.

YARDAGES FOR GUIDANCE

Par	Men	Women
3	up to 250	up to 210
4	251 to 470	211 to 400
5	471 and over	401 to 575
6		576 and over

Flagstick Dimensions

The USGA recommends that the flagstick be at least seven feet in height and that its diameter be not greater than three-quarters of an inch from a point three inches above the ground to the bottom of the hole.

Protection of Persons Against Lightning

As there have been many deaths and injuries from lightning on golf courses, all players, caddies and sponsors of golf are urged to take every precaution for the protection of persons against lightning.

The National Bureau of Standards points out:

"If golf clubs could be impressed with the necessity of calling off matches *before the storm is near enough to be hazardous,* the cases of multiple injury or death among players and spectators could be eliminated."

Raising golf clubs or umbrellas above the head adds to the element of personal hazard during electrical storms.

Metal spikes on golf shoes do little to increase the hazard, according to the Bureau.

Taking Shelter

The following rules for personal safety during thunderstorms are based on material in the Lightning Protection Code, NFPA No. 78-1986; ANSI C5.1-1986 available from the National Fire Protection Association, Batterymarch Park, Quincy, Mass. 02269, and the American National Standards Institute, 1430 Broadway, New York, N.Y. 10018:

a. TYPES OF SHELTER

Do not go out of doors or remain out during thunderstorms unless it is necessary. Seek shelter inside buildings, vehicles, or other structures or locations which offer protection from lightning, such as:

1. Dwellings or other buildings protected against lightning.
2. Large metal-frame buildings.
3. Large unprotected buildings.
4. Automobiles with metal tops and bodies.
5. Trailers with metal bodies.
6. City streets shielded by nearby buildings.

When it is not possible to choose a location that offers better protection, seek shelter in:

1. Dense woods — avoid isolated trees.
2. Depressed areas — avoid hilltops and high places.
3. Small unprotected buildings, tents and shelters in *low* areas — avoid unprotected buildings and shelters in *high* areas.

b. WHAT TO AVOID

Certain locations are extremely hazardous during thunderstorms and should be avoided if at all possible. Approaching thunderstorms should be anticipated and

the following locations avoided when storms are in the immediate vicinity:
1. Open fields.
2. Athletic fields.
3. Golf courses.
4. Swimming pools, lakes and seashores.
5. Near wire fences, clotheslines, overhead wires and railroad tracks.
6. Isolated trees.
7. Hilltops and wide open spaces.

In the above locations, it is especially hazardous to be riding in or on any of the following during lightning storms:
1. Tractors and other farm machinery operated on the golf course for maintenance of same.
2. Golf carts, scooters, motorcycles, bicycles.

Discontinuing Play During Lightning

Attention is called to Rules 6-8 and 33-2d.

The USGA especially suggests that players be informed that they have the right to stop play if they think lightning threatens them, even though the Committee may not have specifically authorized it by signal.

The USGA generally uses the following signals and recommends that all local committees do similarly:

Discontinue Play: Three consecutive notes of siren, repeated.

Resume Play: One prolonged note of siren, repeated.

Lightning Protection for Shelters

Shelters on golf courses may best be protected by standard lightning protection systems. Details on the installation of conductors, air terminals and maintenance requirements are included in the Lightning Protection Code. An alternative method of protection of such shelters is through what is known as providing a "cone of protection" with grounded rods or masts and overhead conductors as described in Section 31 of the Lightning Protection Code. Such a system is feasible for small structures, but probably would be more expensive than a standard lightning rod system.

Down conductors should be shielded with non-conductive material, resistant to impact and climatic conditions to a height of approximately 8 feet to protect persons from contact with down conductors. Shelters with earthen floors which are provided with lightning protection systems should have any approved grounding electrodes interconnected by an encircling buried, bare conductor of a type suitable for such service, or such electrodes should be provided with radial conductors run out to a distance of at least 10 feet from the electrode, away from the shelter.

It is recommended that several notices similar to this be posted at every course. Copies of this notice in poster form may be obtained from the USGA.

RULES OF AMATEUR STATUS

Any person who considers that any action he is proposing to take might endanger his amateur status should submit particulars to the United States Golf Association for consideration.

Definition of an Amateur Golfer

An amateur golfer is one who plays the game as a non-remunerative or non-profit-making sport.

Rule 1. Forfeiture of Amateur Status at Any Age

The following are examples of acts at any age which are contrary to the Definition of an Amateur Golfer and cause forfeiture of amateur status:

1. Professionalism

a. Receiving payment or compensation for serving as a professional golfer or identifying oneself as a professional golfer.

b. Taking any action for the purpose of becoming a professional golfer.

Note: Such actions include applying for a professional's position; filing application to a school or competition conducted to qualify persons to play as professionals in tournaments; receiving services from or entering into an agreement, written or oral, with a sponsor or professional agent; agreement to accept payment or compensation for allowing one's name or likeness as a skilled golfer to be used for any commercial purpose; and holding or retaining membership in any organization of professional golfers.

2. Playing for Prize Money

Playing for prize money or its equivalent in a match, tournament or exhibition.

Note: A player may participate in an event in which prize money or its equivalent is offered, provided that prior to participation he irrevocably waives his right to accept prize money in that event. (See USGA Policy on Gambling for definition of prize money.)

3. Instruction

Receiving payment or compensation for giving instruction in playing golf, either orally, in writing, by pictures or by other demonstrations, to either individuals or groups.

Exceptions:

1. Golf instruction may be given by an employee of an educational institution or system to students of the institution or system and by camp counselors to those in their charge, provided that the total time devoted to golf instruction during a year comprises less than 50 percent of the time spent during the year in the performance of all duties as such employee or counselor.

2. Payment or compensation may be accepted for instruction in writing, provided one's ability or reputation as a golfer was not a major factor in his employment or in the commission or sale of his work.

4. Prizes, Testimonials and Gifts

a. Acceptance of a prize or testimonial of the following character (this applies to total prizes received for any event or series of events in any one tournament or exhibition, including hole-in-one or other events in which golf skill is a factor):

(i) Of retail value exceeding $400; or

(ii) Of a nature which is the equivalent of money or makes it readily convertible into money.

Exceptions:

1. Prizes of only symbolic value (such as metal trophies).

2. More than one testimonial award may be accepted from different donors even though their total retail value exceeds $400, provided they are not presented so as to evade the $400 value limit for a single award. (Testimonial awards relate to notable performances or contributions to golf, as distinguished from tournament prizes.)

b. Conversion of a prize into money.

c. Accepting expenses in any amount as a prize.

d. Because of golf skill or golf reputation, accepting in connection with any golfing event:

(i) Money, or

(ii) Anything else, other than merchandise of nominal value provided to all players.

5. Lending Name or Likeness

Because of golf skill or golf reputation, receiving or contracting to receive payment, compensation or personal benefit, directly or indirectly, for allowing one's name or likeness as a golfer to be used in any way for the advertisement or sale of anything, whether or not used in or appertaining to golf, except as a golf author or broadcaster as permitted by Rule 1-7.

6. Personal Appearance

Because of golf skill or golf reputation, receiving payment or compensation, directly or indirectly, for a personal appearance, except that reasonable expenses actually incurred may be received if no golf competition or exhibition is involved.

7. Broadcasting and Writing

Because of golf skill or golf reputation, receiving payment or compensation, directly or indirectly, for broadcasting concerning golf, a golf event or golf events, writing golf articles or books, or allowing one's name to be advertised or published as the author of golf articles or books of which he is not actually the author.

Exceptions:

1. Broadcasting or writing as part of one's primary occupation or career, provided instruction in playing golf is not included except as permitted in Rule 1-3.

2. Part-time broadcasting or writing, provided (a) the player is actually the author of the commentary, articles or books, (b) instruction in playing golf is not included except as permitted in Rule 1-3 and (c) the payment or compensation does not have the purpose or effect, directly or indirectly, of financing participation in a golf competition or golf competitions.

8. Golf Equipment

Because of golf skill or golf reputation, accepting golf balls, clubs, golf merchandise, golf clothing or golf shoes, directly or indirectly, from anyone manufacturing such merchandise without payment of current market price.

9. Membership and Privileges

Because of golf skill or golf reputation, accepting membership or privileges in a club or at a golf course without full payment for the class of membership or privileges involved unless such membership or privileges have been awarded (1) as purely and deservedly honorary, (2) in recognition of an outstanding performance or contribution to golf and (3) without a time limit.

10. Expenses

Accepting expenses, in money or otherwise, from any source other than from a member of the player's family or legal guardian to engage in a golf competition or exhibition, or to improve golf skill.

Exceptions: A player may receive a reasonable amount of expenses as follows:

1. JUNIOR COMPETITIONS

As a player in a golf competition or exhibition limited exclusively to players who have not reached their 18th birthday.

2. INTERNATIONAL TEAMS

As a representative of a recognized golf association in an international team match between or among golf associations when such expenses are paid by one or more of the golf associations involved or, subject to the approval of the USGA, as a representative in an international team match conducted by some other athletic organization.

3. USGA PUBLIC LINKS CHAMPIONSHIPS

As a qualified contestant in the USGA Amateur Public Links Championships proper, but only within limits fixed by the USGA.

4. SCHOOL, COLLEGE, MILITARY TEAMS

As a representative of a recognized educational institution or of a military service in (1) team events or (2) other events which are limited to representatives of recognized educational institutions or of military services, respectively. In each case, expenses may be accepted from only an educational or military authority.

5. INDUSTRIAL OR BUSINESS TEAMS

As a representative of an industrial or business golf team in industrial or business golf team competitions, respectively, but only within limits fixed by the USGA. (A statement of such limits may be obtained on request from the USGA.)

6. INVITATION UNRELATED TO GOLF SKILL

As a player invited for reasons unrelated to golf skill, e.g., a celebrity, a business associate or customer, a guest in a club-sponsored competition, etc., to take part in a golfing event.

Note 1: Except as otherwise provided in Exception 6 to Rule 1-10, acceptance of expenses from an employer, a partner or other vocational source is not permissible.

Note 2: Business Expenses — It is permissible to play in a golf competition while on a business trip with expenses paid provided that the golf part of the expenses is borne personally and is not charged to business. Further, the business involved must be actual and substantial, and not merely a subterfuge for legitimizing expenses when the primary purpose is golf competition.

Note 3: Private Transport — Acceptance of private transport furnished or arranged for by a tournament sponsor, directly or indirectly, as an inducement for a player to engage in a golf competition or exhibition shall be considered accepting expenses under Rule 1-10.

11. Scholarships

Because of golf skill or golf reputation, accepting the benefits of a scholarship or grant-in-aid other than in accord with the regulation of the National Collegiate Athletic Association, the Association of Intercollegiate Athletics for Women, the National Association for Intercollegiate Athletics, or the National Junior College Athletic Association.

12. Conduct Detrimental to Golf

Any conduct, including activities in connection with golf gambling, which is considered detrimental to the best interests of the game.

Rule 2. Advisory Opinions, Enforcement and Reinstatement

1. Advisory Opinions

Any person who considers that any action he is proposing to take might endanger his amateur status may submit particulars to the staff of the United States Golf Association for advice. If dissatisfied with the staff's advice, he may request that the matter be referred to the Amateur Status and Conduct Committee for decision. If dissatisfied with the Amateur Status and Conduct Committee's decision, he may, by written notice to the staff within 30 days after being notified of the decision, appeal to the Executive Committee, in which case he shall be given reasonable notice of the next meeting of the Executive Committee at which the matter may be heard and shall be entitled to present his case in person or in writing. The decision of the Executive Committee shall be final.

2. Enforcement

Whenever information of a possible act contrary to the Definition of an Amateur Golfer by a player claiming to be an amateur shall come to the attention of the United States Golf Association, the staff shall notify the player of the possible act contrary to the Definition of an Amateur Golfer, invite the player to submit such information as the player deems relevant and make such other investigation as seems appropriate under the circumstances. The staff shall submit to the Amateur Status and Conduct Committee all information provided by the player, their findings and their recommendation, and the Amateur Status and Conduct Committee shall decide whether an act contrary to the Definition of an Amateur Golfer has occurred. If dissatisfied with the Amateur Status and Conduct Committee's decision, the player may, by written notice to the staff within 30 days after being notified of the decision, appeal to the Executive Committee, in which case the player shall be given reasonable notice of the next meeting of the Executive Committee at which the matter may be heard and shall be entitled to present his case in person or in writing. The decision of the Executive Committee shall be final.

Upon a final decision of the Amateur Status and Conduct Committee or the Executive Committee that a player has acted contrary to the Definition of an Amateur Golfer, such Committee may require the player to refrain or desist from specified actions as a condition of retaining his amateur status or declare the amateur status of the player forfeited. Such Committee shall notify the player, if possible, and may notify any interested golf association of any action taken under this paragraph.

3. Reinstatement

a. AUTHORITY AND PRINCIPLES

Either the Executive Committee or its Amateur Status and Conduct Committee may reinstate a player to amateur status and prescribe the waiting period necessary for reinstatement or deny reinstatement. In addition, the Amateur Status and Conduct Committee may authorize the staff of the USGA to reinstate a player to amateur status and prescribe the waiting period necessary for reinstatement in situations where the acts contrary to the Definition of an Amateur Golfer are covered by ample precedent.

Each application for reinstatement shall be decided on its merits with consideration normally being given to the following principles:

(i) AWAITING REINSTATEMENT

The professional holds an advantage over the amateur by reason of having devoted himself to the game as his profession; other persons acting contrary to the Rules of Amateur Status also obtain advantages not available to the amateur. They do not necessarily lose such advantage merely by deciding to cease acting contrary to the Rules.

Therefore, an applicant for reinstatement to amateur status shall undergo a period awaiting reinstatement as prescribed.

The period awaiting reinstatement shall start from the date of the player's last act contrary to the Definition of an Amateur Golfer unless it is decided that it shall start from the date of the player's last known act contrary to the Definition of an Amateur Golfer.

(ii) PERIOD AWAITING REINSTATEMENT

A period awaiting reinstatement of two years normally will be required. However, that period may be *extended or shortened*. Longer periods normally will be required when applicants have played extensively for prize money or have been previously reinstated; shorter periods often will be permitted when applicants have acted contrary to the Rules for one year or less. A probationary period of one year normally will be required when an applicant's only act contrary to the Definition of an Amateur Golfer was to accept a prize of retail value exceeding $400 but less than $10,000.

(iii) PLAYERS OF NATIONAL PROMINENCE

Players of national prominence who have acted contrary to the Definition of an Amateur Golfer for more than five years normally will not be eligible for reinstatement.

(iv) STATUS DURING PERIOD AWAITING REINSTATEMENT

During the period awaiting reinstatement an applicant for reinstatement shall conform with the Definition of an Amateur Golfer.

He shall not be eligible to enter competitions limited to amateurs except that he may enter competitions solely among members of a club of which he is a member, subject to the approval of the club. He may also, without prejudicing his application, enter, as an applicant for reinstatement, competitions which are not limited to amateurs but shall not accept any prize reserved for an amateur.

b. FORM OF APPLICATION

Each application for reinstatement shall be prepared, in duplicate, on forms provided by the USGA.

The application must be filed through a recognized amateur golf association in whose district the applicant resides. The association's recommendation, if any, will be considered. If the applicant is unknown to the association, this should be noted and the application forwarded to the USGA, without prejudice.

c. OBJECTION BY APPLICANT

If dissatisfied with the decision with respect to his application for reinstatement, the applicant may, by written notice to the staff within 30 days after being notified of the decision, appeal to the Executive Committee, in which case he shall be given reasonable notice of the next meeting of the Executive Committee at which the matter may be heard and shall be entitled to present his case in person or in writing. The decision of the Executive Committee shall be final.

USGA Policy on Gambling

The Definition of an Amateur Golfer provides that an amateur golfer is one who plays the game as a non-remunerative or non-profit-making sport. When gambling motives are introduced, problems can arise which threaten the integrity of the game.

The USGA does not object to participation in wagering among individual golfers or teams of golfers when participation in the wagering is limited to the players, the players may only wager on themselves or their teams, the sole source of all money won by players is advanced by the players and the primary purpose is the playing of the game for enjoyment.

The distinction between playing for prize money and gambling is essential to the validity of the Rules of Amateur Status. The following constitute golf wagering and not playing for prize money:

1. Participation in wagering among individual golfers.
2. Participation in wagering among teams.

Organized amateur events open to the general golfing public and designed and promoted to create cash prizes are not approved by the USGA. Golfers participating in such events without irrevocably waiving their right to cash prizes are deemed by the USGA to be playing for prize money.

The USGA is opposed to and urges its Member Clubs, all golf associations and all other sponsors of golf competitions to prohibit types of gambling such as: (1) Calcuttas, (2) other auction pools, (3) pari-mutuels and (4) any other forms of gambling organized for general participation or permitting participants to bet on someone other than themselves or their teams.

The Association may deny amateur status, entry in USGA Championships and membership on USGA teams for international competitions to players whose activities in connection with golf gambling, whether organized or individual, are considered by the USGA to be contrary to the best interests of golf.

CHANGES SINCE 1987

DEFINITIONS

Bunker and Ground Under Repair
Expanded to state that the margin extends vertically downwards, but not upwards.

Casual Water, Loose Impediments and Obstructions
Amended to state that manufactured ice is an obstruction.

Stroke
Expanded to state that, if a player checks his downswing voluntarily before the clubhead reaches the ball, he is deemed not to have made a stroke.

RULES

3-3. Stroke Play; Doubt as to Procedure
Amended to provide that (1) a competitor is not obligated to report the facts to the Committee if he scores the same with both balls and (2) if a competitor fails to announce in advance his decision to invoke this Rule or his selection, the score with the original ball, rather than the higher score, will count.

4-1g. Clubs: Damage
Amended to prohibit further use during a round of a club which ceases to conform because of damage sustained other than in the normal course of play.

4-2. Clubs: Playing Characteristics Changed
Amended to distinguish between the playing characteristics of a club being changed as a result of damage sustained in the normal course of play and other than in the normal course of play.

4-4. Maximum of Fourteen Clubs
Amended to allow the addition or replacement of a club by borrowing from another person playing on the course.

5-3. Ball Unfit for Play
A stricter definition as to what constitutes a ball unfit for play has been adopted.

6-8. Discontinuance of Play
Former Rule 6-8b dealing with the procedure when play is discontinued has been replaced by a sub-section (Rule 6-8b) on the procedure when play is suspended by the Committee and a sub-section (Rule 6-8c) on lifting the ball when play is discontinued during play of a hole.

13-2. Improving Lie, Area of Intended Swing or Line of Play
Expanded to prohibit improving the area in which a ball is to be dropped or placed.

15-1. Playing a Wrong Ball: General
Amended to provide that a ball substituted under an applicable Rule which does not permit substitution is not, as previously was the case, a wrong ball. Corresponding changes have been made in the Definitions of "Ball in Play" and "Wrong Ball," and in Rule 20-4.

16-2. Ball Overhanging Hole
Amended to provide that if a ball overhanging the hole falls into the hole after the time limit has expired, the player incurs a penalty stroke and is deemed to have holed out with his last stroke.

18-2b. Ball Moving After Address
Amended to require replacement of a ball which moves after address. Previously, the ball was played as it lay. As a result of this change, a ball which moves or is moved in all circumstances covered by Rule 18 must be replaced.

19. Ball in Motion Deflected or Stopped
Amended to apply solely to accidental deflection of a ball. Purposeful deflection is dealt with under Rule 1-2.

19-5. Ball in Motion Deflected or Stopped by Another Ball
Expanded to provide the procedure if two balls in motion collide.

21. Cleaning Ball
Amended to state that a lifted ball may be cleaned except in three specified circumstances. Previously, the circumstances in which a lifted ball may be cleaned were listed.

25-1b(ii)(b), 25-1c(ii)(b), 26-1b and 28c. Dropping Ball Behind Condition
Amended to state that the ball must be dropped keeping the point where the ball lay (or where it last crossed the margin of the hazard) between the hole and the spot on which the ball is dropped. Previously, it was permissible to stand on that line and drop the ball an arm's length to either side.

34-1b. Claims and Penalties: Stroke Play
Amended to state the two situations in which a penalty of disqualification shall be imposed after the competition is closed.

Appendix I
LOCAL RULES

Ball Drops
Expanded to authorize establishment of a "Ball Drop" when it is not practicable to proceed in conformance with the ground under repair Rule.

USGA ASSOCIATION MEMBERSHIP

USGA Associate membership lets everyone know you've made an investment which brings great returns to everyone who plays the game of golf.

As a USGA Associate, you're helping the USGA keep golf the way you love it. And you are part of a nationwide network of dedicated golfers. You also receive special amenities, including a year of *Golf Journal*, the *Rules of Golf*, and other exclusive membership benefits.

You can become a USGA Associate for only $25 or you can choose a higher level with even more benefits. A USGA Associate membership also makes a perfect gift. Join at the highest level you can. You'll enjoy your USGA Associate investment for years to come.

Call Today, 1-800-223-0041, or send in the coupon below.

—Arnold Palmer
National Chairman
Associates Program

Yes, I want to invest at the following level:

☐ ASSOCIATE $25   ☐ EAGLE CLUB $100
☐ ASSOCIATE Husband & Wife* $30   ☐ EAGLE CLUB Husband & Wife* $125
☐ JUNIOR Under 18 $15

Your Name_____

Address_____

City_____State_____Zip_____

Friend's name to be enrolled in the level checked above:

Name_____

Spouse* (if applicable)_____

Address_____

City_____State_____Zip_____

Enclosed is my check payable to USGA Associates Program for $_____

☐ Charge my: ☐ American Express   ☐ Visa   ☐ Master Card

_____
Card Number   Expires

Signature_____

Mail this coupon to: USGA Associates Program, Golf House, Far Hills, NJ 07931